# Nothing Rhymes with Orange

## A Children's History of Orange County

# THIS BOOK PROUDLY OWNED BY

This book is made possible
by the generous contributions of the following:

*Angels Baseball*
*The Disneyland Resort®*
*Kaiser Permanente*
*Ingram Micro*
*SchoolsFirst Federal Credit Union*
*AT&T*
*Anaheim Ducks and the Honda Center*
*Metrolink*
*UPS*

**Nothing Rhymes With Orange**
Tesoro Publishing
Post Office Box 528
Fullerton, California 92836
www.tesoropublishing.com

ISBN 978-0-9797419-8-2   0-9797419-8-X

Second Edition, November 2011

Every effort has been made to produce a dependable history book based on information gathered from news articles, reference books and interviews. Although every attempt was made to be as accurate as possible, Tesoro Publishing does not make any representation that this book is free from error.

Tesoro Publishing supports educational programs and students by contributing to scholarships and local schools.

Nothing Rhymes with Orange
Authored by Stan Oftelie
Cover Design by Dan Almanzar
Book Design and Illustration by Dan Almanzar
Back Cover Photo from www.ASliceInTime.com

Library of Congress Catalog Card Number: application pending

Printed in the United States of America

# A Children's History of Orange County

By
## STAN OFTELIE

Illustrated By
## DAN ALMANZAR

Tesoro Publishing
Fullerton, California
2011

# Author's Note

To help young readers learn new vocabulary words, some of the challenging words in *Nothing Rhymes with Orange* are printed in **boldface**. All **boldfaced** words are listed in alphabetical order and briefly defined in the Glossary beginning on page 265. The Glossary, like a dictionary, is a key to unlocking the meanings of new words.

Also, each chapter of *Nothing Rhymes with Orange* ends with a **replica** of one of the orange crate labels that once advertised Orange County to the world and a brief profile of a person who helped shape the place we live in today.

There are 29 profiles in this book. Hundreds of people could have been profiled, but these 29 people had a significant and lasting impact on Orange County's past and future.

# Table of CONTENTS

**C**ONGRATULATIONS!

You are about to learn more about Orange County, California than probably anyone in your family or in your neighborhood. This book was written by Stan Oftelie, who uncovered information that will make third grade history fun and exciting. After reading it, you will be a superstar of knowledge about Orange County.

You will discover some interesting facts and I'll bet if you go home and share them with your family members and friends, they will be surprised by what you know! For example, did you know that Orange County was part of Mexico a long time ago? You and your classmates will also learn about street names, city names, and places of interest in Orange County. You will discover the "Secret Club," and you may want to start one in your own class.

I think the most fun part of this amazing history book is that as you drive around Orange County with your family, you will be able to teach them about street names and places you visit. It might even be fun for you to plan a trip around Orange County where you share clues with your family and have them guess where they're going. History can be fun, and I know you will find *Nothing Rhymes with Orange* as enjoyable as I did. We are very fortunate to live in Orange County, a place that is filled with history and opportunities!

*William M. Habermehl*

William M. Habermehl
Orange County Superintendent of Schools

# The Un-rhymable Word

Miss Jones stood next to her desk, **adjusted** her eye glasses, and smiled at her third grade class.

"Who knows what country we live in?" she asked.

Hands shot up everywhere. Miss Jones looked at a serious little girl holding her arm straight up, waggling her hand in the air.

"Katie?" the teacher said.

"We live in America," Katie said. "The United States of America, the USA."

"U-S-A! U-S-A!" chanted Christopher, a third grader with a goofy smile and a mop of brown hair. He had heard the USA chants when he watched sports shows on television.

Miss Jones frowned and told Chris to raise his hand when he had something to say. His big smile got a little bit smaller, but it would not disappear.

Miss Jones had another question for the class.

"Who knows what state we live in?" she asked.

Fewer hands went up, but Katie knew that answer, too.

"California," she said confidently. Sometimes Katie came off like a Miss Know-It-All, but she usually knew the right answers.

"That's right," Miss Jones said. "We all live in California."

The teacher asked if anyone knew what city they lived in. Almost every hand in the class room went up.

That was an easy question, but Miss Jones followed it up with a hard one.

"Does anyone know what county we live in?"

There was silence in the classroom. No one said anything. No one moved. No one knew what a county was.

The teacher waited, then said, "We live in Orange County—a place some call The OC."

"We live in a very important county," Miss Jones said.

Orange County's nickname is The OC

"There are more than three million people living here. Only two California counties have more people than Orange County and, in terms of where people live, Orange County is the sixth biggest county in America. The OC is a very big and important place."

"Today," the teacher said, "Orange County is a place filled with homes and families and schools. We have great shopping malls and freeways and 34 different cities.

"But if we go back in time, Orange County was a very different place.

"Once there were dinosaurs and saber-toothed tigers here," she said. "Years later came Indians, brave Spanish explorers, an Old Mission era and the time of the **ranchos.** Later, Orange County was part of the Old West, with cowboys and **saloons** and gunfights.

"Over time, Orange County became one of the world's richest farming areas—a place where families grew their own food and lived near sweet-smelling **citrus** groves. Even a President of the United States lived on a lemon ranch here when he was a third grader."

Miss Jones stopped, fiddled with her glasses, and looked at Chris.

"Christopher," she said. "Do you know how Orange County got its name?"

Chris **squirmed** in his seat.

"From oranges?" he said with a pained look on his face.

Orange County's population is bigger than 20 states

"Good thought," said Miss Jones. "Oranges are a part of our history, but only one part. This year we will learn a little bit about oranges and a little bit about how Orange County got its name and a lot about our local history."

"History is boring," Chris said, looking down. His smile was completely gone.

"I don't think so," said Miss Jones. "I think you will see that history is alive all around us—in our county's street names, in our cities, and in things we see every day.

"Disneyland is part of our history," she said. "So are Knott's Berry Farm and our beautiful beaches. I think

you'll see that our local history helps make Orange
County a very special place, a place that is different
from every other place in the world."

Chris flashed a big, **mischievous** smile. "There is one
other thing that makes Orange County really, really
special," he said.

"What's that?" asked Miss Jones, forgetting that Chris
did not raise his hand.

"It's the word orange," he said. "Nothing rhymes
with orange."

*For 70 years, orange crate labels advertised
Orange County to the world.*

**Walt Disney**
**(1901-1966)**

Walt Disney founded a global entertainment empire built on his cartoons, his television shows, his live-action feature films and his world-class theme parks.

He also created some of the world's most famous cartoon characters, including Mickey Mouse, Minnie Mouse, Donald Duck, Goofy and Pluto.

Walt Disney built Disneyland in Anaheim and called it "The Happiest Place on Earth."

When he opened his Magic Kingdom, he invented the family-friendly amusement park experience and created what today is Orange County's largest private employer.

Walt Disney World in Florida, and Disneylands in Tokyo, Paris and Anaheim are all named for him. Disney Way in Anaheim and three elementary schools, one in Anaheim, one in Burbank, and one in Missouri, also honor him.

Thinking about the un-rhymable word was driving Katie crazy. Something had to rhyme with orange.

Sitting in the backseat of her mom's Ford minivan, Katie ran through the letters of the alphabet, trying out every letter with the word orange. Borange didn't work. Neither did *corange* or *dorange*. Nothing worked. No real word rhymed with orange.

Joaquin is pronounced *"wah-KEEN"*

Katie thought about the rhyme while her mom drove her and her little brother Niko to a dinosaur exhibit in Buena Park. Niko loved dinosaurs, but Katie knew she would be bored while Niko looked at giant fake lizards and some old duck-billed dino bones.

The little dinosaur **exhibit** was at Ralph B. Clark Regional Park. It was better than Katie expected.

9

There weren't any fake lizards, all the **fossils** were real and all the dinosaur bones were from Orange County.

The exhibit had a big painting showing woolly mammoths with curved tusks fighting. The mammoths looked like hairy elephants. There was a big glass display case with a life-sized saber-toothed tiger skeleton attacking a life-sized camel skeleton.

And the featured exhibit was a huge, nine-million-year-old skeleton of a giant prehistoric baleen whale named Joaquin.

The bones of the ancient whale were cool. They were found on a Laguna Niguel hillside years ago when road builders were constructing the San Joaquin Hills toll road.

Katie wanted to know how a giant whale like Joaquin got buried on a hill so far from the ocean, so she asked a park ranger.

The helpful ranger explained that when Joaquin was alive, all of Orange County was underwater. When Joaquin died millions of years ago, the huge whale dropped to the bottom of the ocean, and over time he was buried in dirt and sand.

About 10,000 years ago, the ranger explained the weather changed, the ocean fell back and what is now South Orange County became dry land. Joaquin never moved. The coastline and the sandy beaches moved, leaving Joaquin, the prehistoric whale, buried in what had become an inland hillside.

Katie looked at the park ranger and asked what *prehistoric* was.

The ranger said prehistory was the time before anyone wrote things down, a time before there was any real written history.

Without anything written down, the park ranger said, **archaeologists** pieced together a lot of little clues to re-create the ancient world of prehistory, the same way they pieced together a lot of fishy fossils to re-create a giant whale like Joaquin.

It was a good story, but even with the ranger's little talk, it did not take Katie very long to look at everything in the little dinosaur exhibit. She was losing interest and was ready to go home.

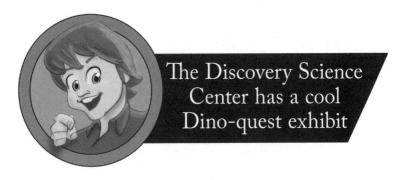

The Discovery Science Center has a cool Dino-quest exhibit

However, Niko the Nikosaurus wasn't ready to go home. He was staring google-eyed at a prehistoric sloth fossil. He wasn't even blinking. Katie knew he would have a meltdown if they tried to leave, so she plopped down all alone on a green bench by the door.

She began thinking about the un-rhymable word. She ran through the alphabet again, matching each letter with the word orange.

Katie said each nonsense word in a quiet voice: *Aorange. Borange. Corange. Dorange.*

"Wait a minute," she said out loud.

*Dorange.*

That was it.

The next day, Katie asked Miss Jones if she could tell the class about the dinosaur exhibit.

Katie talked about Orange County being underwater for millions of years and the woolly mammoth painting and the nine-million-year-old bones of a giant whale named Joaquin.

"And," she said, "I thought of something that rhymes with orange."

Chris perked up. Miss Jones looked surprised.

"The word that rhymes with orange," she said, "is door hinge."

*Lithographed labels were pasted on the end of wooden citrus boxes.*

**Ralph B. Clark**
**(1917-2009)**

Ralph Clark was an Orange County Supervisor for 16 years and once was mayor of Anaheim.

He served as Chairman of the Orange County Transit District (OCTD) Board of Directors 14 times, helping to build one of America's finest public bus systems.

When Ralph Clark joined the brand new OCTD Board in 1971, Orange County had no buses and no passengers. Today's Orange County Transportation Authority carries 63 million bus trips a year on a 565-bus transit system.

He also helped bring the Los Angeles Rams professional football team to Angel Stadium in 1980. The Rams played 15 seasons in Orange County before moving to St. Louis, Missouri.

Ralph B. Clark Regional Park in Buena Park is named in his honor.

RALPH B. CLARK REGIONAL PARK
8800 ROSECRANS AVENUE

# 3 Arrow-Proof Vests

Chris did not like it when Katie rhymed the un-rhymable word. He didn't know why. He just didn't like it.

At first, he thought Katie cheated by using two words to make the rhyme. He even thought about complaining that orange and door hinge really did not rhyme very well at all, which was true.

But Chris decided to say nothing, just to smile. He planned to tell a joke that would be awesome if he could keep from blurting it out too soon. It was hard not to say something right away, but he just had to wait. Timing was everything.

While Chris was thinking about prehistoric whale fossils and his cool joke, Miss Jones was talking about Orange County's prehistoric people, the people who came here about 5,000 years ago, long before there were any written records of their lives.

Today we call these people Native Americans or American Indians.

Many were undisturbed for thousands of years. They still were living **Stone Age** lives in their little villages when a Spanish explorer named Gaspar de Portolá arrived. His 62-man expedition, with some men on foot and some on horseback, ventured into what is now Orange County.

In 1769, Portolá's Spaniards were exploring the lands between San Diego and San Francisco, looking for places to build forts they called *presidios*, towns they called *pueblos* and churches they called *misiónes*, or **missions**. They wanted to build a mission at a place they called San Juan Capistrano.

The barefoot Native Americans, who did not wear very many clothes, **gawked** when the heavily-dressed, well-armed Spaniards walked into their primitive villages. The Spanish *conquistadores* carried big, thick swords and steel-tipped spears. They had leather boots on their feet and metal helmets on their heads.

And the Spanish soldiers were wearing special jackets and vests—some of them six cow hides thick—so they would not be hurt by arrows with stone arrowheads.

"They were wearing bullet-proof vests, only for arrows," said Chris.

Miss Jones said Chris was right, but that he should raise his hand before speaking. She knew Chris was paying attention and thinking about what she was saying.

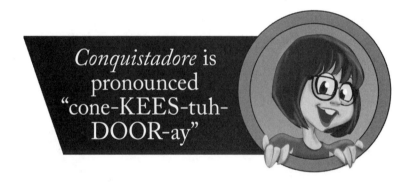

*Conquistadore* is pronounced "cone-KEES-tuh-DOOR-ay"

Miss Jones said a Spanish priest named Father Juan Crespi kept a diary of Portolá's expedition, writing about the beautiful places they saw and their exciting adventures. It was the first written description of the land that would become Orange County.

One of the soldiers described in Father Crespi's diary was Sgt. José Francisco de Ortega, the brave pathfinder who rode ahead of Portolá's expedition to look for food and to find the best—and safest—places to set up camp.

19

Over the years, Sgt. Ortega returned to San Juan Capistrano many times.

In 1775, he brought two large church bells to San Juan Capistrano. When he was suddenly called to San Diego to help fight an Indian **uprising**, Sgt. Ortega and his conquistadores had to bury the mission bells so they could not be stolen or turned into metal-tipped arrows or other deadly weapons.

A year later, Sgt. Ortega returned to San Juan Capistrano, helped dig up the buried bells, and helped build a big **adobe** bell tower so the sounds of the church bells could be heard for miles.

Laura Hoffman

*Mission bells still ring at the Mission San Juan Capistrano today.*

On November 1, 1776—All Saint's Day—the mission bells were ringing when a Franciscan Father named Junípero Serra, the spiritual leader of all California Catholics, dedicated the Mission San Juan Capistrano as the seventh of California's 21 missions.

Big and beautiful, the mission at San Juan Capistrano became known as *The Jewel of the Missions.*

Today, California's oldest buildings are at the Mission San Juan Capistrano. Father Serra's chapel at the mission is California's oldest church.

*This old drawing depicts the Mission San Juan Capistrano in the late 1700s.*

Chris thought Miss Jones was a good storyteller when she talked about the old mission and the buried church bells, but he did not pay much attention when she talked about dates or years. All the numbers just seemed to jumble together.

Because Chris did not pay attention to numbers, he was a little surprised when Miss Jones said that the Mission San Juan Capistrano was founded on the West Coast in 1776—the same year that General George Washington and American patriots were fighting the Revolutionary War 3,000 miles away on the East Coast.

Chris had never thought about what was going on in his home town while an important event like the American Revolution was going on somewhere else.

Ortega Highway is named after Francisco de Ortega

For the first time, he stopped to think about it: In 1776, while the American Colonists were fighting the British Redcoats, Spaniards were building a famous mission near his future home.

Kind of cool, Chris thought.

*In the 1930s, a girl feeds the birds at Mission San Juan Capistrano.*

For some reason, Chris liked it when Miss Jones said the California missions supported General Washington and the American Revolution.

The missions sent money to the Americans to help fight the British. Mission San Juan Capistrano sent the American **rebels** $223.

Laura Hoffman

It was not a lot of money, but Chris still felt a little proud when he realized some people from where he lived helped out during America's War for Independence.

It was the same kind of good feeling that he had when he watched the fireworks and listened to patriotic songs on the Fourth of July—America's Independence Day.

When Miss Jones said it was time to go outside, Chris realized that he was so busy thinking about 1776 and the Mission San Juan Capistrano and the American Revolution, he forgot to tell his cool joke in class.

He missed his chance.

As his class headed outside, Chris realized it would be hard to tell his funny fish story at just the right time.

This could be tough.

*Gaspar de Portolá is depicted with a flag of Spain.*

Gaspar de Portolà
(1716-1784)

A nobleman who served as Captain of the Spanish Dragoons during wars in Italy and Portugal, Gaspar de Portolá became an explorer for King Carlos III of Spain and founded the New World Alta California pueblos at San Diego and Monterey.

The first Spanish **military** governor of California, he led a 1769 expedition of trailblazing explorers who marched from San Diego to San Francisco.

Portolá and his men were the first Europeans to see the San Francisco Bay and also the first to see the land that would become Orange County.

The well-respected explorer also was the governor of the Puebla region of Mexico from 1776 until his death in 1784. Orange's Portola Middle School and Portola Parkway in Irvine and Lake Forest are named for him.

# 4 Pirates of the Coast

Chris was looking for the perfect time to tell his fish story when he realized he was telling more of a fish joke than a fish story.

Actually, he was trying to find a way to fix up a somewhat lame fish joke his dad told him. Chris thought he could change the fish joke around a little to make it funny.

He would tell his fish joke about Joaquin, the whale fossil that Katie talked about. It would crack everyone up.

Everyone but Katie, he thought. Nothing made her laugh. She always seemed **annoyed**.

By telling a joke about something he heard in class, Chris thought he could make the lame fish joke funny. He just had to find the right time to spring his story.

Chris was thinking about the timing for his joke while Miss Jones was talking about the Mission San Juan Capistrano's Great Stone Church.

In a time of adobe and wood buildings, the Franciscan Fathers dreamed of building a Great Stone Church that would become California's most **magnificent cathedral**.

But in 1812 violent earthquakes left the Great Stone Church in ruins.

Miss Jones said that Spain's King Carlos would not pay to repair the Great Stone Church. Spain was fighting a long and expensive war with Mexican rebels, and the King did not have enough money to repair a crumbling mission in faraway California.

First American

*Father Lucius Zither stands by an Old Mission archway.*

Like the colonists who came to America from England and then fought to take control of their lives, the Spanish colonists in Mexico did not want to be told what to do by a distant ruler. Rather than pay **taxes** to Spain, the Mexican rebels wanted their own government.

For more than ten years, the Mexican rebels fought with King Carlos's Spanish soldiers.

In 1818, while Mexico and Spain fought, a French pirate named Hippolyte de Bouchard and his Argentine buccaneers **ransacked** the California coast, pillaging pueblos and missions, stealing silver, gold and other treasures.

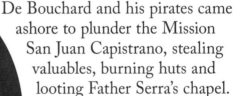

De Bouchard and his pirates came ashore to plunder the Mission San Juan Capistrano, stealing valuables, burning huts and looting Father Serra's chapel.

Some said the pirates did more damage to the mission than the 1812 earthquakes.

While the San Juan Mission suffered, Mexican rebels finally won their long war with Spain in 1821. A year

*Hippolyte de Bouchard*

later, the Mexican flag was raised over the Mission San Juan Capistrano, and all the land that would later become Orange County was a part of Mexico.

When the war between Mexico and Spain was over, the Spanish soldiers and many of the Franciscan Fathers left their presidios, pueblos and missions and returned to Spain.

Miss Jones said some Spanish families stayed in what would become Orange County because King Carlos gave them large gifts—some called land grants—that were perfect for raising sheep and cattle. The new Mexican government also gave out big land grants.

By the 1840s, more than 20 big land grants—called ranchos—had been granted in what is now Orange County. Miss Jones had a map showing the old land grants.

## Orange County's Historic Ranchos

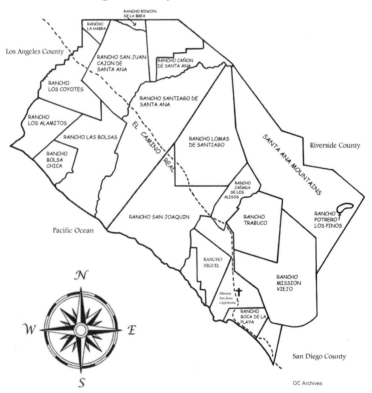

OC Archives

There were no freeways or landmarks on the map, so it was hard to figure out where things were. But Miss Jones showed them about where their school was located.

Once Chris saw where his school was on the map, he was able to figure out about where his house was on an old land grant. Chris thought it was cool that he lived on what once a great cattle ranch.

Miss Jones talked about life on the dusty old ranchos, about cattle branding, about cowhides being tanned into leather, and about sheep being sheared to make wool blankets and heavy cloth.

Orange County was a part of Mexico from 1821 to 1848

Miss Jones described how sleek Yankee sailing ships soon were coming ashore all along the California coast to trade their **manufactured** metal goods like spoons, knives, door hinges, hammers and nails for the *rancheros'* cowhides and wool blankets.

Katie perked up when Miss Jones mentioned door hinges. But when she realized that the teacher was not going to rhyme orange with door hinge, Katie went back to daydreaming about white-sailed **windjammers** gliding gracefully over the ocean a long, long time ago.

The tall ships were special to Katie. She had seen them before, in her real life.

*Charles Chapman's famous Old Mission brand*
*was founded in 1897.*

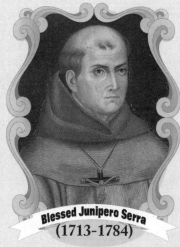

**Blessed Junipero Serra**
**(1713-1784)**

Father Serra, a Franciscan **friar** sometimes called the Apostle of California, was the founder and builder of California's missions, including the Mission San Juan Capistrano.

Named the *Father Presidente of California Missions* in 1767, the Majorca-born Father Serra was a professor of philosophy in Spain before he came to the New World to convert Native Americans to Christianity.

He was accused by some of using harsh methods in his dealings with Native Americans, but few challenged his deep commitment to his religious faith.

In 1988 he was **beatified** by Pope John Paul II, a step towards sainthood in the Catholic Church.

Junipero Serra Road and JSerra Catholic High School in San Juan Capistrano are named in his honor.

# 5 Cowhides Spinning like FRISBEES

Katie saw her first three-masted sailing ship at Disneyland.

It was a replica of the famous windjammer *Columbia*, a 1787 sailing ship. Katie saw the sailing ship on the same Frontierland waters as the big *Mark Twain* riverboat. She thought the *Columbia* looked like a pirate ship.

When she went on Disneyland's *Columbia* ride, Katie did a little exploring.

Below deck, the sailing ship had a little **nautical** museum, with a spyglass and an **astrolabe**. She was surprised at how small the sailors' living spaces were.

On deck, she could see the ropes and rigging and the white canvas sails. The ship's masts were very tall. She counted ten heavy cannons on the sides of the sailing ship and heard the ship's bell ring loudly as it cruised around Tom Sawyer's Island.

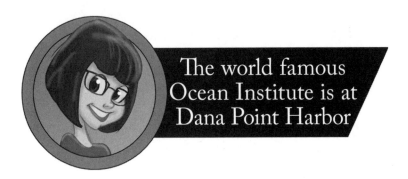

The world famous Ocean Institute is at Dana Point Harbor

The *Columbia* was great, she thought, but it did not match the brig *Pilgrim*.

Katie had seen a life-sized replica of the original *Pilgrim* in Dana Point Harbor when her mom picked up her cousin Diego. He had been staying overnight on the *Pilgrim* as part of an Orange County Ocean Institute program.

As a fifth grade greenhand, Diego swabbed the *Pilgrim's* deck, stood night watch and learned a sea chantey, which is a special sailors' song. He did not get much sleep on the tall ship, but he had a great time.

Katie got to go on board the *Pilgrim* when they picked up Diego. Katie thought it was wonderful. The *Pilgrim* was like the *Columbia*, but somehow it seemed more real.

Because she had seen tall ships with her own eyes, Katie was very interested when Miss Jones started talking about how the real-life *Pilgrim* traded Yankee manufactured goods for cowhides with the rancheros living near Mission San Juan Capistrano.

*The* Pilgrim *heads for Dana Point.*

Ocean Institute

In 1835, the *Pilgrim's* crew included a talented teenager named Richard Henry Dana, Jr., a boy sailor who wrote a vivid **journal** describing the ship's voyages and adventures.

After trading with San Juan Capistrano rancheros, sailors hauled the heavy hides to a steep cliff above a sandy beach. With the stiff cowhides stacked on the edge of a high cliff, Dana and the other sailors threw the hides to the beach.

Some of the stiff cowhides would spin like Frisbees, some would sail like kites and a few got caught on rocks or tangled up in scrub brush partway down the steep cliff.

The sailors had to get every cowhide to the *Pilgrim* or they would be punished by their rough-and-tough captain. To get stray cowhides, the sailors tied ropes around young Dana and lowered him down the steep cliff to retrieve stuck hides.

The young sailor wrote that he was very frightened as the sailors lowered him down the cliff face, swinging him so he could shake loose every cowhide. Dana was terrified.

"I could see nothing below me but the sea and the rocks upon which it broke and a few gulls flying in mid-air," he wrote. Despite his fear, Dana retrieved every cowhide.

He later wrote that after the *Pilgrim's* captain traded with the rancheros, the heavy hides were loaded onto the ship, taken halfway around the world and then sold to New England factories. The California cowhides became leather shoes, boots and saddles.

After two years as a seafaring man, Dana returned to New England and turned his journal into a book, *Two Years Before the Mast*. His book became a best seller. Some people say it is the best book ever written about sailors' hard lives at sea.

*Two Years Before the Mast* made Richard Henry Dana, Jr. a rich man. Miss Jones said his tales of spinning cowhides to the beach and dangling by ropes over the rocks and the surf were the first published descriptions of the area that would become Orange County.

Over time, the high, steep cliff face where Richard Henry Dana, Jr. once threw hides to the beach would become known as Dana Point. An Orange County city is also called Dana Point. Dana Point Harbor is the home port of the replica of the brig *Pilgrim*, where Katie's cousin Diego once had an overnight adventure.

San Juan Capistrano Historical Society

*Sculptor John Terken stands by a miniature version of his Richard Henry Dana, Jr. statue.*

39

And above today's Dana Point Harbor stands a 9-foot-tall bronze statue of a young Richard Henry Dana, barefoot and shirtless like a 19th century sailor, holding his journal and looking out to sea. It is a tribute to the famous writer and sailor.

Katie listened carefully and quietly as Miss Jones talked about Richard Henry Dana, Jr.'s statue and the *Pilgrim* and cowhides spinning off bluff tops. She loved the stories.

*Two Years Before the Mast* was a popular 1946 movie

But Chris was all fidgety. He wanted to tell his fish story, but felt his chances were slipping away. He had to do something fast.

He decided to try his fish story out on Katie when the class went outside.

As they left the classroom, Chris ran up to Katie and asked her about the giant whale fossil named Joaquin. He said Joaquin sounded like he was bigger than 100 pianos.

"What do pianos have to do with anything?" an annoyed Katie asked.

"You can tune a piano," Chris said, "but you can't tune a fish."

He flashed his big goofy smile.

"Get it?" he said. "Tune a fish? Tuna fish? You can tune a piano but you can't tuna fish."

Katie got it. She was even more annoyed.

"Whatever," she said.

Dumb, she thought.

Chris was disappointed. He thought that if he had told the tuna fish story in front of the whole class when Katie first talked about Joaquin the whale, everyone would have laughed. He had waited too long to tell his story.

And, he thought, Katie didn't laugh at his joke because she was just a sourpuss. *A big sourpuss.*

As he went outside, he thought about the word *sourpuss*. He liked the way it sounded. He said it out loud.

Cool word, *sourpuss*.

*Sunkist, the world's biggest citrus cooperative, featured windjammer art.*

**Richard Henry Dana, Jr.**
**(1815-1882)**

A sailor, lawyer, politician and author of the 1840 classic book, *Two Years Before the Mast*, Richard Henry Dana, Jr. was a leader in abolishing slavery in the United States.

The son of a Yankee poet also named Richard Henry Dana, the younger Dana graduated from Harvard Law School and was elected to the Massachusetts State Legislature. He served briefly as America's Ambassador to Great Britain.

Before the American Civil War, attorney Dana argued against the federal **Fugitive** Slave Law. He defended runaway slaves regularly in Massachusetts courts. He was an early supporter of Abraham Lincoln's presidential campaign.

Dana Point Harbor and the City of Dana Point are named for Richard Henry Dana, Jr.

# 6 Panning for GOLD

Miss Jones was looking down her nose into a little bottle of water with glittering gold flakes at the bottom. Her glasses and the water in the little bottle enlarged her eye to twice the size of her other eye. It made her look funny.

Chris wasn't laughing. He usually enjoyed it when a teacher looked a little silly, but not this time. He was not laughing. He was excited.

"It's real gold," Chris said as the teacher peered into his little bottle.

Chris had volunteered to share his little gold strike after Miss Jones first described how prospectors called 49ers panned for gold in cold streams and shallow rivers during California's Gold Rush.

After Miss Jones first talked about prospectors and California's Gold Rush, Chris told her that he once panned for gold, too. He found his gold at Knott's Berry Farm.

Chris told Miss Jones that a prospector at Knott's, a guy wearing a beat-up old cowboy hat, a red flannel shirt and suspenders, helped him swirl a gold-mining pan in a little stream of water until a few flecks of gold were glittering in the bottom of his pan.

OC Archives

*Panning for gold at Knott's Berry Farm.*

The prospector put Chris's gold dust and some water into a little bottle called a vial. Chris got to take the vial home. He told Miss Jones he could bring his little vial of gold and water to school to prove his story.

When Miss Jones said he could tell his story to the class, Chris smiled his biggest, goofiest smile. He could hardly wait.

The next day, while Chris daydreamed about gold, Miss Jones talked about a man named James Marshall and how he discovered gold nuggets near John Sutter's Northern California lumber mill in 1848.

Marshall made his great gold find in the closing days of America's war with Mexico, which was a war over land and the boundaries between Mexico and the United States.

While **diplomats** were writing a peace treaty—an agreement later known as the Treaty of Guadalupe Hidalgo—James Marshall and mill owner John Sutter were trying to keep their 1848 gold strike a secret.

Over time, the diplomats found a way to make their peace, but Marshall and Sutter could not find a way to keep their golden secret.

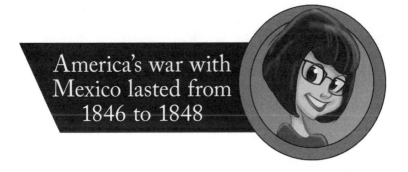

America's war with Mexico lasted from 1846 to 1848

When word of the gold strike at Sutter's Mill leaked out, thousands of people from all over the world were gripped by gold fever. They rushed to California to strike it rich. The Gold Rush was on.

Between 1848 and 1852, California's population grew from about 14,000 people to more than 223,000 people. Miss Jones said the gold seekers pouring into California came from every corner of the world. They were called 49ers because so many arrived in 1849.

While talking about the gold-hungry 49ers, Miss Jones looked at Chris. She told the class that San Francisco's pro football team was called the 49ers because of the 1849 Gold Rush.

Chris liked sports teams. He knew about the San Francisco 49ers. He did not try to memorize dates, but, because of the San Francisco 49ers football team, he always remembered the California Gold Rush was in 1849.

Knott's Scary Farm's
Halloween Haunt
started in 1973

While Miss Jones talked, Chris was getting nervous. He wanted to tell the class about panning for gold, but the teacher kept talking about the California Gold Rush.

Chris knew he had to wait until it was his turn to talk, but waiting made him fidgety.

While Chris squirmed, Miss Jones said the Treaty of Guadalupe Hidalgo ended the United States' war with Mexico and let the Mexican rancheros keep their ranchos.

Most of the sleepy Southern California ranchos were dry, dusty, cattle-grazing land, far from Northern California's high-spirited gold hunters, she said. The Southern California ranchos were afterthoughts in the peace treaty.

Miss Jones said most of the 49ers went to Northern California to get rich quick but never found any gold. Only a few became rich. Most ended up empty-handed and broke.

Miss Jones paused. She told the class that even if only a few of the 49ers found gold, she knew someone who found some real gold at Knott's Berry Farm. She asked Chris to share his gold panning story with the class.

Chris was ready. He spoke in a strong, clear voice. He passed around his little vial with gold flakes at the bottom while he talked, so everyone would know his story was true.

While they looked at the gold dust in his little vial, Chris talked about swirling his pan in the little stream near Knott's Boot Hill graveyard. He talked about looking into a jail cell where a spooky, wood-carved character named Sad-Eye Joe talked to

OC Archives

*Sad-Eye Joe*

49

him and knew his name. He talked about the old prospector who helped him.

When Chris finished his story, Miss Jones was holding his little bottle of clear water and gold dust. Everyone in the class had gotten to see it and hold it. Miss Jones held it up for everyone to see it.

"During the California Gold Rush, thousands of people came to Northern California to find gold like this," she said. "But very few 49ers came to Southern California, because there was no gold here."

Then Miss Jones made an **astonishing** statement.

"In Orange County," she said, "some people believe that water, like the water in this little bottle, is actually more valuable than all the gold in Northern California."

*Argonauts were seafaring adventurers,*
*like the gold-seeking 49ers.*

**Walter Knott**
**(1889-1981)**

A Buena Park berry farmer, Walter Knott and his wife Cordelia began serving specially seasoned fried chicken at a roadside restaurant in 1934.

The Chicken Dinner Restaurant was so popular that he built an exact copy of an Old West Ghost Town, complete with a wagon camp, a schoolhouse and a gold-panning attraction, to entertain the customers waiting long hours for their dinners.

In 1966, Knott built a replica of Philadelphia's Independence Hall at Knott's Berry Farm. It was his tribute to the signing of the Declaration of Independence and the U.S. **Constitution**.

Knott Avenue and Knott's Berry Farm are named in his honor.

# 7 Bamboozled

Katie did not believe water was more valuable than gold. It didn't make any sense to her.

Plenty of water came out of water fountains or out of a hose. People watered their lawns. Water was not rare or valuable. Katie thought that even the little bit of gold in Chris's bottle had to be worth more than water.

Katie thought Miss Jones might be trying to pull a fast one on the class for some reason. It had to be some sort of trick. Katie was going to figure it out.

Katie was not going to be **bamboozled** by anyone.

But Miss Jones was serious when she talked about the value of water.

She described terrible **droughts** in the days after California became the 31st state in the union on September 9, 1850.

Because there was no rain and little water on the great ranchos, cattle died of thirst and sun-scorched crops dried up in the fields. The sun-bleached white bones of dead cattle were everywhere.

Early Anaheim was called *Campo Alemán*– The German Camp

With no cowhides to trade and no beef to sell, many of the once-rich rancheros became desperate for money to pay their bills and their taxes.

Their troubles became worse when the U.S. Congress disputed the Treaty of Guadalupe Hidalgo and told the rancheros that they had to prove they owned their own land.

The rancheros hired lawyers, looked for old records, and tried to prove they owned their land. Many could not prove they received **valid** land grants. Some lost everything.

One Mexican ranchero who fought his way through the American legal system was Juan Pacifico Ontiveros, the owner of the *San Juan Cajon de Santa Ana*, a rancho that includes today's cities of Brea, Fullerton, Placentia and part of Anaheim.

Juan Pacifico's 36,000-acre rancho was vast, but it was not very good for cattle grazing. Miss Jones said Ontiveros dismissed much of his dry land as *peor que nada*—an old Spanish phrase meaning "worse than nothing."

Without life-giving water, his dry, flat, cactus-choked rancho was not worth very much money at all.

However, in 1857, a bearded, Austria-born surveyor named George Hansen came to the Ontiveros rancho, saying he wanted to buy some dry land for the Los Angeles **Vineyard** Society, a group of German immigrants.

Hansen and another Vineyard Society leader named John Fröhling offered to buy more than 1,000 acres of Don Juan Pacifico's land if they could also dig a six-mile long **irrigation ditch** from the Santa Ana River to the Vineyard Society property.

*George Hansen*

Rather than relying on rain water, the irrigation ditch would give them a reliable supply of water for grape growing.

With plenty of water available, surveyor Hansen believed the German wine-making **community** would thrive.

Don Juan Pacifico, who believed Hansen and Fröhling wanted to buy worthless land that "couldn't support a goat," quickly agreed to sell. He took his money and moved north. He left the rest of *Rancho San Juan Cajon de Santa Ana* to his sons.

Anaheim is
Orange County's
oldest city

While George Hansen was drawing up plans, planting the first grapevines and supervising the digging of the irrigation ditch, the charter members of the Los Angeles Vineyard Society, including John Fröhling, Conrad Kuchel, and Charles Kohler, met and voted on a name for their new town.

Miss Jones said most of the Los Angeles Vineyard Society wanted to use the German word for home—*heim*—in the town's name. They also wanted to recognize the value of Santa Ana River water, so they added Ana to the first part of the new town's name.

By only a two-vote margin, the Los Angeles Vineyard Society named its new town Anaheim. The runner-up was Anagau, with *gau* being a German way of describing a river region. Anagau, and not Anaheim, almost became the town's name.

As Miss Jones talked about early Anaheim, Katie realized how important water was for cattle and crops. Water was like gold to the ranchers and farmers and would be like gold for generations to come.

Katie thought about water and the dying cattle and the six-mile long irrigation ditch between Anaheim and the Santa Ana River. Without water, there would be no Anaheim, no grape-growing, no cattle-grazing—just dry, dusty land where a goat could not survive.

*Anaheim workers make cement irrigation pipes in about 1908.*

For some people, water really could be as valuable as gold. Katie understood what Miss Jones meant when she held up Chris's little bottle of clear water with gold dust in the bottom. Water was valuable. Maybe as valuable as gold.

Katie was sure she was not being bamboozled.

She thought for a moment.

Cool word, *bamboozled.*

*In 1925, the Gold brand was a popular trademark of Villa Park's Central Lemon Association.*

**Helena Modjeska**
**(1840-1909)**

Actress Helena Modjeska was Orange County's first international celebrity.

One of the world's most famous actresses, she left Poland in 1876 to create a **utopian** farming community in Anaheim.

Her plans to create an agricultural paradise did not work out. She didn't know anything about farming.

To earn a living, Madame Modjeska learned English and returned to the stage. She toured the world as an actress, but she always returned to her Orange County home.

Susan Sontag's **fictionalized** version of Madame Modjeska's life, called *In America*, won the National Book Award in 2000.

A statue of Helena Modjeska stands in Anaheim's Pearson Park. Her Modjeska Canyon home, which she called Forest of Arden, is a county regional park.

# 8 TWILIGHT of the Ranchos

Chris was thinking about secrets and mysteries.

Miss Jones told her class she would reveal secrets when she talked about local history. So far, Chris thought the teacher had not let them in on any secrets. She was just talking about old, ancient stuff. He was getting bored.

Maybe, he thought, he had missed something.

So Chris listened very carefully when Miss Jones said that when the Los Angeles Vineyard Society bought land that would become the City of Anaheim, it really signaled the **twilight** of the great ranchos.

California was the 31st state to join the Union

She said life on the ranchos began to change even before California became a state.

By 1850, an English sea captain named John Foster and an American hide trader named Abel Stearns, both

61

married to Mexican women, began buying ranchos and creating cattle-grazing empires.

She talked about the great ranchos with beautiful Spanish names. She described how the man who was once called John Foster became known as Don Juan Forster and put together a gigantic 200,000-acre ranch, a ranch so big you could see it from the moon.

As Miss Jones talked, Chris's mind was spinning. He was getting a headache. A dull headache.

He tried to pay close attention, but Spanish ranch names didn't mean a thing to him. He couldn't care less about Don Juan Forster's 200,000-acre ranch or some dead guy named Abel Stearns. And he didn't have any idea how big 200,000 acres were. No idea at all.

There weren't any unrevealed secrets in Miss Jones's talk, just lists of old cattle ranches and old cattle ranchers.

Boring.

Just plain boring.

Chris put his cheek into the palm of his right hand. His fingers covered his right eye and his eyebrow. He started thinking about soccer practice.

First American

*Abel Stearns*

Miss Jones could see Chris was not paying attention. She talked about the **swashbuckling** Don Jose Andreas Sepulveda's coastal rancho, his fine clothes and his love of gambling. Chris was looking straight ahead. He was not listening.

After talking about how ranchos were getting bigger and bigger, it was time for a break. As the class headed outside, Miss Jones stopped Chris and asked him what was wrong.

At first, Chris said nothing was wrong.

Abel Stearns was called *Cara de Caballo Viejo* or "Old Horseface"

Miss Jones asked if he was learning a lot about local history.

Chris did not say anything. He was uncomfortable talking to his teacher this way.

He took a breath. He said he wanted to learn some hidden secrets about local history, but he really had not learned any. He was interested in explorers and the Gold Rush and the Portolá expedition, but just a little interested. It was just okay, not really great stuff.

He certainly was not hearing anything mysterious or secret.

Chris took a deep breath.

"A lot of this stuff is boring," he said, a little afraid that he would make his teacher mad.

Miss Jones was not angry. She looked at Chris seriously. She remembered how excited he was when he talked about his panning-for-gold experience and when he found his house on a map of old ranchos. He was interested then, but not now.

Miss Jones once told the class they would enjoy local history when they saw that it was alive all around them. So far, Chris was not seeing it.

Chris was starting to think that local history was about dull, dead guys and their property. And there was a dizzying list of dates that did not mean anything. There was nothing magical about any of it. There were no amazing secrets.

"Christopher, you've given me a good idea," Miss Jones said. "It means we jump a little bit ahead, but I think it will help make our magical local history come alive for everyone.

"And I think it will let you in on a few secrets."

She smiled.

"We'll talk about it with the entire class when everyone comes back inside."

*Artist Archie J. Vazquez designed the Tesoro box-end label.*

# How Big Was Don Juan Forster's 200,000-Acre Rancho?

Let's compare yesterday's great rancho to today's Orange County landmarks.

| Landmark | Size in Acres |
|---|---:|
| 1. Orange County Fairgrounds | 150 acres |
| 2. Angel Stadium, including parking lots | 160 acres |
| 3. Knott's Berry Farm | 160 acres |
| 4. California State University, Fullerton | 236 acres |
| 5. Disneyland Resort | 500 acres |
| 6. John Wayne Airport | 500 acres |
| 7. Mile Square Regional Park | 640 acres |
| 8. Bolsa Chica Ecological Preserve | 1,000 acres |
| 9. University of California, Irvine (UCI) | 1,000 acres |
| 10. La Palma, Orange County's smallest city | 1,016 acres |
| 11. City of Irvine's Great Park | 1,347 acres |
| 12. Crystal Cove State Park | 2,761 acres |
| 13. Seal Beach Naval Weapons Depot | 5,256 acres |
| 14. Laguna Coast Wilderness Area | 6,500 acres |
| 15. The three-county Chino Hills State Park | 14,372 acres |
| 16. Irvine, Orange County's largest city | 44,800 acres |
| 17. Donald L. Bren's open space land donations | 50,000 acres |
| 18. Cleveland National Forest (Orange County portion only) | 70,000 acres |

**All 18 Combined** . . . . . . . . . . . . . . . . . . . . . . **199,476 acres**

**Juan Forster**
(1813-1882)

Adventurer John Foster was a sea captain and a hide trader when he first came to California in 1833.

Three years later, he changed his name to Juan Forster and married the beautiful Ysidro Pico, sister of Pio Pico, the Mexican Governor of California. Forster became a citizen of Mexico.

With Governor Pico's help, Don Juan Forster became California's biggest landowner. At one time, his 200,000-acre ranch stretched south from today's City of Lake Forest to the City of Oceanside in San Diego County.

The Forster family has remained active in Orange County for generations. A San Juan Capistrano Middle School is named for his great-grandson, Marco Forster. Today, the Forster mansion in San Juan Capistrano is a national landmark.

THE
FORSTER MANSION
A NATIONAL
HISTORIC LANDMARK

Miss Jones stood next to her desk and flashed a big smile. Katie thought she was up to something.

"When I finish talking about the great ranchos, I'm going to have a special local history assignment for you," she said. "I think you'll enjoy it."

Chris was disappointed and just a little mad. He wanted to learn some secrets, not get more homework. He hated homework. This wasn't fair.

Still, he had to focus and pay attention. Miss Jones might give some clues about the special assignment when she talked about the ranchos.

Chris listened carefully when Miss Jones said that after California became a state, American **investors** began to buy land in what is now Orange County. Big investors wanted to raise sheep and cattle. Small investors wanted to start family farms or businesses.

She said a San Francisco grocery store owner named James Irvine and his business partners, Llewellyn Bixby and Bixby's cousins, Benjamin and Thomas Flint, were among the big investors. Irvine, Bixby and the Flints were sheepmen, raising thousands and thousands of sheep, and then shearing their wool to make cloth.

During the American Civil War, when the Union could not buy cotton from the Southern states, the Flint Bixby Company sold wool to the federal government to make blue uniforms for the Union Army. They made a fortune.

Wool uniforms are warm but very itchy

With the money they made, they bought more and more land so they could raise more and more sheep. In December of 1864, the Flint Bixby Company bought José Andreas Sepulveda's *Rancho San Joaquin*.

After a long drought and after a plague of crop-eating grasshoppers, neighboring rancheros were forced to sell their land to the Flint Bixby Company. The company's sheep grazing empire grew to 125,000 acres.

In 1876, James Irvine bought out his partners in the Rancho San Joaquin and, over time, the sheep-grazing property became known as the Irvine Ranch. Bixby and the Flints continued to raise sheep on their other lands.

First American

*Cowboys shear sheep for wool.*

Land baron Abel Stearns also was squeezed financially during the drought years, just like the old rancheros. When he died in 1871, Stearns's family could not pay his bills or his taxes, so they sold Abel Stearns's land to farmers and small investors to pay off old debts.

While small investors were buying little pieces of the Stearns lands, big investors were buying huge chunks of land. The biggest investors were Irishmen James Flood and Richard O'Neill.

Flood, the man called "Nevada's Silver Baron," and his old friend, cattleman O'Neill, bought the last great rancho in what would become Orange County—the lands once owned by Juan Forster.

"Today, the O'Neill property—still called Rancho Mission Viejo—is Orange County's last great cattle ranch," said Miss Jones. "It has rodeos and fiestas and real-life cowboys. It is a beautiful place where Orange County's ranching heritage really comes alive."

San Juan Capistrano Historical Society

*Cowboy Joaquin Errecarte with a branding iron.*

Chris looked up at his teacher when Miss Jones talked about history really coming alive.

Miss Jones made direct eye contact with Chris.

"Now I have a special assignment for all of you," she told the class. "I want you to solve a puzzle first. You can ask anyone you want for help.

"Here's the puzzle," she said. "There's a street that is next to Disneyland and the Honda Center and the Los Alamitos Race Course and Angel Stadium. What street is it? And the second part of the assignment: What's special about this street?"

Chris stared at Miss Jones without even blinking.

What did a street next to Disneyland, a hockey arena, the ballpark and a racetrack have to do with anything?

Disney©

Anaheim Public Library

Los Alamitos

ANGEL STADIUM ANAHEIM

Anaheim Public Library

He didn't get it.

When Chris later learned the answer to the first part of the mysterious puzzle, it didn't help one bit.

Not one bit.

*In the 1940s, Los Angeles's Schmidt Litho crafted this Irvine Ranch lithograph.*

**James Irvine**
**(1827-1886)**

Teenager James Irvine fled Ireland's 1845 potato famine to find work in New York paper mills. In 1849, he headed west to California to find gold.

Rather than making his fortune in the goldfields, James Irvine made big money selling supplies like picks, shovels and gold mining pans to other miners.

He used his **profits** to open a very successful Gold Rush–era grocery business in San Francisco. He used his grocery store profits to buy real estate, including the immense San Joaquin Ranch.

He later named his vast sheep-grazing land the Irvine Ranch.

The City of Irvine, as well as streets, schools, and parks, are named for James Irvine, the Irvine family and the Irvine Ranch.

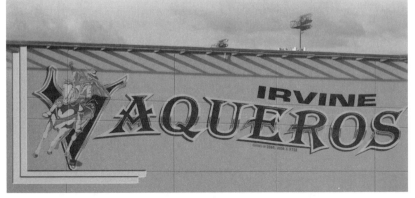

# 10 New Towns, Gnarly Whiskers

Chris's dad knew what street was next to Disneyland, the Honda Center, Angel Stadium and the Los Alamitos Racetrack: Katella Avenue.

But when Chris asked what was special about Katella Avenue, his dad didn't say much.

"Katella's a busy street," Chris's dad said. "Lots of cars. Lots of traffic."

Laura Hoffman

*Heavy traffic motors down Katella Avenue.*

That was no secret, Chris thought. His dad always complained about traffic. Too many cars on an Orange County street was not the answer to a mysterious riddle.

Chris had half an answer. He knew Katella was the street in the puzzle, but that was all he knew. He didn't know anything special about a long, busy street with lots of cars.

When he went back to school, Chris was fidgety when Miss Jones did not ask for the puzzle solution right away. She wanted to talk about new cities first. Chris tried to be patient and **concentrate** on what she was saying, but he was a little jittery.

Miss Jones started by reminding the class that although Anaheim was planned in 1857, it did not become a full-fledged city until 1870, when Anaheim became the first real city east of the San Gabriel River.

Orange County has 34 different cities

Miss Jones paused for a moment, and then explained that when California became a state in 1850, all of what is now Orange County was a part of Los Angeles County. The county was run by five men called the Los Angeles County Board of Supervisors.

The elected supervisors were very powerful. For towns to become full-fledged cities, they needed the supervisors' permission.

If the supervisors thought a town had enough people and enough tax money to pay its bills, they could allow a local cityhood election. If the supervisors did not want an election, none was held. Anaheim was the first town

Alana Cacciatori

in what is now Orange County to get the supervisors' permission to become a full-fledged city.

In the late 1860s, after the American Civil War ended, other towns began popping up in what was then called southeast Los Angeles County. Many of the new towns wanted to become big-time cities.

First American

*Columbus Tustin*

Miss Jones said new towns called Richland, Tustin City and Santa Ana were formed east of the Santa Ana River. Over time, Richland became Orange, Tustin dropped the word City from its name, and Santa Ana grew until it had more people than any other Orange County city.

Tustin City was named after a Philadelphia buggy builder named Columbus Tustin, a gold-hungry 49er who did not strike it rich as a miner, but who made a lot of money as a custom carriage maker.

Tustin, with a partner named Nelson Stafford, bought 1,359 acres of sycamore trees and wild mustard east of the Santa Ana River. They planned to sell bits of land to farmers and to build a new town on their new property.

Beginning in 1868, the balding, hard-working Columbus Tustin tried to **organize** a town on his share of the land. He did not do very well.

Tustin Tiller Days celebrates Tustin's farming past

Tustin tried giving away land to bring businesses to his town. Few businessmen took the free land. Tustin opened a post office and was appointed postmaster. He convinced Wells Fargo to have a stage coach deliver mail to his town, but a new post office did not attract new people.

Tustin did not have enough water to attract farmers or businesses. And without a reliable source of water, there was not much mail or many people coming to Tustin City. Still, Columbus Tustin kept **promoting** his little town.

Water was also an issue for another former 49er, a wild-whiskered general-store owner named William H. Spurgeon. Spurgeon and his business partner,

*William H. Spurgeon*

Major Ward Bradford, started a town they called Santa Ana, which was not far from Tustin City.

Chris could not stop looking at photographs of Bill Spurgeon.

"Crazy beard on that dude," Chris said. "Gnarly whiskers."

If Miss Jones heard Chris, she ignored him. She continued with her story.

Like Tustin City, Miss Jones said, Santa Ana started slowly. The weird-bearded Spurgeon opened a general store. He became Santa Ana's postmaster. He wrote letters asking old friends to move to his new town. He

*Jenny and Bill Spurgeon pose in front of their general store.*

81

tried giving away land to bring in homeowners and businesses, but no matter how hard he tried, very few people moved to Santa Ana.

When Santa Ana's growth stalled, the impatient Major Bradford sold his share of the land and moved to San Diego. Spurgeon—called Uncle Billy by nearly everyone—stayed and tried to make Santa Ana the best city in the Santa Ana Valley. He did not have much luck, but he kept trying.

Nearby, two well-known Los Angeles attorneys, Alfred B. Chapman and Andrew Glassell, made plans for a town they called Richland.

Chapman and Glassell supported the South during the Civil War

After the American Civil War, lawyers Chapman and Glassell did some legal work to untangle the confusing finances of the old rancheros. Rather than getting paid money for their legal work, the attorneys were paid in land.

Chapman and Glassell did a lot of legal work and got a lot of land, including a spot they thought would be perfect for a new town.

They wanted to call their town Richland, but when the post office told them that the name Richland was already taken, the attorneys renamed their new town Orange.

To set their town apart, they designed a distinctive downtown traffic circle that became known as the Orange Plaza.

*Alfred Chapman*

Chris was zoning out on old names, new towns and dead guys with gnarly beards when Miss Jones paused. She took a deep breath.

"Think about some of the names I just mentioned: Tustin, Glassell, Chapman, even Spurgeon," she said. "And names we talked about earlier, names like Ortega and Portolá.

Joe Oftelie

"These names are a part of our history," she said. "And they are alive today in street names and school names and city names, not just in the pages of dusty old history books. When you look, you see these names—and others like them—every day."

Chris knew Miss Jones was saying something important. He listened carefully.

"Here's a secret," Miss Jones said. "When you know these names and you connect them to people who shaped our local history, you know things that most people don't know.

"And when you know the special connection between the people who shaped our local history and the Orange County we live in today, you become very special. Your special knowledge makes you a member of a very special Secret Club."

*Andrew Glassell*

Miss Jones let what she said sink in for a moment.

"There's magic in knowing things that other people don't know," she said. "Knowing about our local history

unlocks secrets and lets you join the Secret Club."

Chris was trying to decide if what Miss Jones was saying was cool or not. He liked knowing secrets and being in a Secret Club, but he wasn't sure if it was really *magic*. Magic was a pretty big deal.

84

Before he decided what he thought, the teacher began talking about her special assignment. Chris was jarred. He started thinking about Katella Avenue.

"Let's talk about the puzzle I gave you," she said. "First, what street runs by Disneyland, Angel Stadium, the Honda Center and the Los Alamitos Race Course?

Los Alamitos Race Course is in Cypress, not Los Alamitos

"And, second, what makes the street special?"

Miss Jones smiled.

"The answers illustrate a one-of-a-kind Orange County secret."

Chris's head was spinning. Was there some famous guy named Katella that he didn't know about? Did Miss Jones talk about this Katella guy when he wasn't paying attention?

Then another, even scarier, thought began bouncing around in his head.

What if that Know-It-All Katie knew the answer?

Author's Collection

*Blue Goose was a marketing rival of Sunkist Growers.*

**Richard O'Neill**
**(1824-1910)**

Richard O'Neill was a Boston butcher when he caught gold fever in 1849.

He did not find his fortune in the goldfields, but, over time, he opened a San Francisco meat market and befriended two Irish saloonkeepers, James Flood and William O'Brien.

Flood and O'Brien invested in Nevada silver mines, struck it rich and became two of the wealthiest men in America.

Over time, James Flood asked his old friend Richard O'Neill to run a big cattle ranch. It **prospered**. Later, Flood asked O'Neill to manage a much bigger ranch, promising to give him half the ranch if it made money, too. In 1906, Flood's family kept the old promise and deeded O'Neill half of the old Forster Rancho.

O'Neill Drive in Ladera Ranch, O'Neill School, and O'Neill Regional Park are named for the O'Neill family.

As Miss Jones asked her first question, Chris was looking at Katie out of the corner of his eye.

"Who knows what street is next to Disneyland, the Honda Center, Angel Stadium, and Los Alamitos Race Course?" Miss Jones asked.

Chris raised his hand. A dozen other hands shot up, too. Katie's arm went straight up in the air, but she was not waggling her hand at the teacher.

No waggle, Chris thought.

A good sign.

While Chris thought about Katie's waggling hand, Miss Jones called on him. She did not call him Christopher. She did not say that she made the assignment after Chris told her history was boring.

Chris tried to sound confident as he answered.

"Katella Avenue is the street next to those places," he said.

Miss Jones smiled. Chris was right. He smiled his big, goofy smile.

"What's special about Katella?" Miss Jones asked.

No one moved. Chris did not raise his hand. Neither did Katie. Neither did anyone else.

Laura Hoffman

Miss Jones smiled again.

"I'm going to tell you a secret," she said. "Katella is a made-up word, a special word an Anaheim rancher named John B. Rea invented in the 1890s—more than a century ago."

Miss Jones said rancher Rea had two young daughters—Kate and Ella—and he combined their first names into a single, made-up word: Katella. He called his walnut groves the Katella Ranch.

Over time, the made-up word Katella became famous.

Anaheim Public Library
*The Rea sisters*

A dirt road leading to the Rea's ranch became known as Katella Road. The dusty dirt road became a paved Anaheim street. When other cities connected their streets to Katella Road, it became a major avenue in six cities.

When John Rea helped organize an elementary school district near his ranch, the little school district was called Katella, too.

In 1966, Miss Jones said, an Anaheim high school was named after the little school district, and famous athletes, big businessmen, and two members of Congress— Republican Ed Royce and Democrat Loretta Sanchez— graduated from Katella High.

Laura Hoffman

*Kate and Ella statues located near Disneyland.*

Miss Jones smiled and said the origin of the name Katella was a mystery to most people. They may have heard the word or seen it on road signs, but they didn't know where it came from or what it meant.

"Now you know," Miss Jones said. "You know a local history secret. You are members of the Secret Club."

Mash the names Kate and Ella together and you get Katella, Chris thought. Kind of cool.

Being in the Secret Club was cool, too.

*Ed Royce*
*Member of Congress*

*Loretta Sanchez*
*Member of Congress*

Chris was thinking about the Secret Club when he saw Miss Jones' mischievous smile.

"Now," she said, "you have to find some local secrets for me. If you want to earn extra credit and earn a special place in the Secret Club, you have to solve a local mystery."

Miss Jones had a stack of 3x5 index cards in her hand. She passed the cards out as she explained the assignment.

"There are 34 cities in Orange County," she said. "There's a city name written on each card. You must find a local history secret about the city on your card, something hidden in the names of your city's streets, or parks or schools."

Miss Jones explained a little more.

"If your city was Stanton, for example, you could say Katella is a big street in Stanton and tell me the story of Kate and Ella," she said. "Katella is an example of our past being alive and people not knowing its secret. That's what you are looking for."

Chris was holding the 3x5 index card with Stanton written on it.

Sweet, he thought.

This should be easy. He just had to write up something about the two farm girls named Kate and Ella and the big street in Stanton.

Then Miss Jones changed the rules.

"I've already told you about Kate and Ella," she said, "so you can't use my secret for your city. You have to find your own secret."

Chris was not happy. He didn't know anything about Stanton. He had never heard of it.

This might not be so easy after all.

Lemons were a major crop for the huge La Habra Citrus Association.

**Dr. Arnold O. Beckman**
**(1900-2004)**

Corona del Mar's Arnold O. Beckman is Orange County's most famous scientist.

A member of the National Inventors Hall of Fame, he holds 14 classic patents for his discoveries, including the pH meter to test citrus acidity and the spectrophotometer, a device that revolutionized chemical analysis.

He was a pioneer investor in Silicon Valley semiconductor research and founded Beckman Coulter, Inc., a scientific corporation based in Brea.

A charity he created, the Arnold and Mabel Beckman Foundation, has given more than $400 million to scientific research and education.

UCI's Beckman Laser Institute, Caltech's Beckman Laboratory of Chemical Synthesis and Irvine's Arnold O. Beckman High School are named in his honor.

# 12 A COMMOTION in Class

While Miss Jones's class looked at the city names written on their blue-lined 3x5 cards, the teacher began talking about Orange County government.

While Miss Jones talked, Katie was reading the words Villa Park on her card over and over again. She was going to find a secret about the city. She would find something good.

She was determined to get a special spot in the Secret Club.

As Katie looked at the words *Villa Park*, Miss Jones said that settlers in the towns of Anaheim, Santa Ana and Orange first tried to escape from Los Angeles County in 1869.

"Counties were created by the California Constitution in 1852," Miss Jones said. "The Constitution wrote down important state laws and gave counties important duties, including protecting property, helping poor people, providing public health services, overseeing the courts and providing law enforcement in county territory."

She stopped.

"How many of you have ever heard of a sheriff?" Miss Jones asked.

Almost every hand in the room went up.

Chris **mumbled** something about the Sheriff of Nottingham and Robin Hood, but Miss Jones did not hear him.

Today, Orange County government has 17,895 employees

Instead, she smiled at all the hands up in the air, said "Good!" and told the class to put their hands down. She kept on talking.

"The sheriff protects the public, arrests bad guys and runs the jails," she said. "The district attorney is the county lawyer who **prosecutes** accused criminals and, if they are found guilty, sends them off to jail or prison. The sheriff and district attorney are crime fighters who are a part of county government.

"Another important elected official is the assessor, who decides the value of property for taxes," the teacher said, "and the elected clerk-recorder, who makes sure real estate **transactions** are reported honestly and issues marriage licenses and birth certificates.

"There are other important countywide elected officials—the auditor, the treasurer, the coroner, the tax collector and the superintendent of schools, the county's elected education leader," Miss Jones said. "But the best-known county elected officials are the board of supervisors, who run the county."

Anaheim Public Library

*Early Anaheim settlers bottle wine at the Bullard Winery.*

She said early settlers in Anaheim, Santa Ana, Tustin and Orange did not like the way the Los Angeles County Board of Supervisors ran their county. They thought the supervisors ignored them.

The early settlers said the only time Los Angeles County officials paid any attention to them was when

Los Angeles needed money. When they needed money, the supervisors raised everyone's taxes.

After the supervisors got their hands on the tax money, the settlers believed their tax dollars went to improve roads near Los Angeles or to hire sheriff's deputies to protect people in Los Angeles.

The settlers felt they got nothing for their tax money.

They saw only bad roads near their homes and bold bandits who knew there were no sheriff's deputies around to stop criminals. The settlers did not like it.

They wanted to see their taxes used to improve their own towns, not faraway Los Angeles.

The settlers had other complaints. They did not like day-long, horse-and-buggy rides to Los Angeles

*Cover of an 1888 brochure promoting the City of Orange*

to conduct routine county business, like filing legal documents, recording deeds or getting a birth certificate.

They did not like Los Angeles—or the Los Angeles County Board of Supervisors—one bit. They wanted a government that paid attention to them. *They wanted their own county.*

Miss Jones said that between 1869 and 1889, the settlers tried at least six times to convince the State Legislature to form a new county in southeast Los Angeles County. Every try failed.

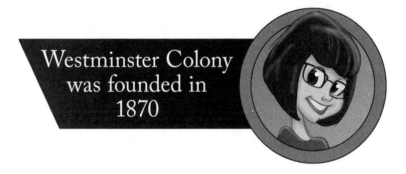

Westminster Colony was founded in 1870

She said the State Legislature rejected a plan for an Anaheim County and another plan for a Santa Ana County. The State Legislature refused four different plans to carve a county called Orange out of southeastern Los Angeles County.

Miss Jones said no one really knew exactly why the early pioneers finally settled on the name Orange County when they tried to create a county, but she said local historians had a pretty good idea of why the name was chosen.

"Orange was picked as the perfect county name long before there was a City of Orange or even before the first **commercial** orange groves were planted here," Miss Jones said.

Miss Jones said local historian Jim Sleeper believes the name Orange County was chosen as part of a clever scheme to attract new farmers to the area.

First American

*Families worked together to can and preserve home grown fruit in the 1890s.*

"Smart farmers knew you needed a warm, mild **Mediterranean climate** to grow oranges," she said. "Mr. Sleeper said the name Orange County was chosen to make farmers think the weather here would be perfect for orange growing."

The name Orange County was perfect, she said, but despite the perfect name and the perfect climate, the California Legislature would not create a new county.

Miss Jones paused.

"In 1889, things changed," she said. "Two important Santa Ana men—the town's founder, the man they called Uncle Billy Spurgeon, who was a Democrat, and his friend, a Republican named James McFadden—went to the State Capitol to try to convince the legislature to create Orange County.

"They were very successful."

As soon as Miss Jones said the word *successful*, Katie let out a big, loud, honking laugh.

Miss Jones was startled.

Katie's face turned red, but she still had a big smile on her face. Katie was giggling.

Chris was amazed. Katie never disrupted the class. Not her. She was a stone-faced sourpuss.

Miss Jones was not pleased. She was surprised that it was Katie causing a **commotion**. Katie never caused a disturbance. Never.

But Katie knew something they did not know: Sometimes things look really funny backwards.

OC Archives

*Consolidated Orange Growers operated in Orange
from 1930 through 1965.*

**James McFadden**
(1842-1919)

A New York-born investor and a millionaire Republican businessman, college-educated James McFadden was the political boss of the Santa Ana Valley for more than 25 years.

In the 1890s, McFadden and his brothers built a railroad line between their Santa Ana lumberyard and their Newport Beach wharf, connecting ocean-going ships with major inland rail lines. The transportation connection allowed the McFaddens to become Southern California's lumber barons.

A **prohibitionist** and behind-the-scenes political powerhouse, James McFadden served for years on the California Republican Central Committee.

He provided the political muscle needed to push through the 1889 state law creating Orange County.

Santa Ana's McFadden Intermediate School and McFadden Avenue in Santa Ana, Westminster and Huntington Beach are named in his honor.

# 13 The BACKWARDS TRICK

Katie caused the commotion because she practiced being a good reader.

Katie liked to read and wasn't afraid to read out loud. She had a big vocabulary. She was good at sounding out words.

And she read all the Junie B. Jones books and all the Allie Finkle books, simply because she liked reading.

Katie even knew a few reading tricks.

She knew how to use the glossary in the back of a book to learn new words. When she learned a new word, she tried to use it in a sentence later that day—even if the word sounded funny, like *bamboozle*.

Portfolio.com says Newport Beach is America's richest city

To practice sounding out words, one of her tricks was to write a word backwards and then try to pronounce it, even if it was a nonsense word. Sometimes when you said something backwards, you got something funny sounding.

Her name backwards—K-a-t-i-e—became E-i-t-a-k, a word she pronounced eye-tak. The boy sitting next to her—Lee Berry—was Yrreb Eel. She called him Eel once. He looked at her like she was crazy. Her teacher, Miss Sarah Jones, was Senoj Haras Ssim backwards. It was the card that Miss Jones—or Senoj Ssim—handed out that *really* caused the commotion.

While she was half-listening to her teacher talk about counties, Katie looked at the words Villa Park and sounded them out backwards.

Villa Park backwards was *Krap Alliv.*

Crap Alive.

As soon as she realized the backwards name, she laughed her loudest honking laugh— and disrupted her teacher and her class.

"What's wrong, Katie?" asked Miss Jones in her stern school teacher voice.

"Nothing," said Katie. She was embarrassed and she could feel her face getting red, but she still had a big grin on her face. Krap Alliv was pretty funny.

Miss Jones was not amused.

"Do you want to share something?" asked Miss Jones sharply.

Katie thought for a moment. The backwards name was pretty funny. Everyone would laugh, but Miss Jones wouldn't like it. Katie thought it was better not to say anything.

"No," she said. "I don't have anything to share."

Katie's face was very red now.

"We'll talk later," Miss Jones said. The tone in her voice was serious.

Katie was really, really embarrassed. She was no longer smiling. She felt bad.

With just a hint of a frown, Miss Jones described how James McFadden and Bill Spurgeon convinced the State Legislature to let local people vote on splitting away from Los Angeles County.

*An early map of Orange County also features a **cornucopia** of farm products.*

Voters—all of them men because women could not vote in 1889—approved the creation of Orange County on June 4th by an overwhelming 2,509 to 500 vote.

Forty-three days later, voters went to the polls again. They chose Santa Ana as the county seat—the capital of Orange County. Voters also elected the first board of

*Dick Harris,
first sheriff of
Orange County*

*E.E. Edwards,
first district attorney
of Orange County*

supervisors and key officials, including a sheriff and a district attorney.

First American

*In 1890, the McFadden brothers built a railroad
between their Newport harbor wharf and Santa Ana.*

Miss Jones said Orange County was born on August 5, 1889, when the first chairman of the first board of supervisors—Uncle Billy Spurgeon of Santa Ana—called the first supervisors meeting to order.

After twenty years of trying, Orange was a county.

When she said it, Miss Jones did not seem very happy about Orange becoming a county. The teacher seemed a little upset—or at least a little grumpy.

Katie knew Miss Jones wasn't unhappy about Orange becoming a county.

Katie knew her teacher was unhappy with her.

*In 1921, Anaheim was called
the Capital of the Valencia Orange Empire.*

**William H. Spurgeon**
**(1829-1915)**

William H. Spurgeon founded the City of Santa Ana and was Orange County's first **prominent** politician.

The Kentucky-born Spurgeon was a Southern Democrat elected to the Los Angeles County Board of Supervisors in 1876 and elected to the California State Assembly in 1886. He was the first mayor of Santa Ana.

He was elected to the first Orange County Board of Supervisors in 1889 and served as the first chairman of the board.

During his lifetime, the wild-whiskered William Henry Spurgeon was a beloved figure, called "Uncle Billy" by friends and foes alike.

Spurgeon Street in Santa Ana, Spurgeon Intermediate School and two Spurgeon Parks—one in Santa Ana and one in Newport Beach—are named in his honor.

# 14 The OC's OLD WEST

When the class went outside, Miss Jones said she wanted to talk to Katie.

Katie was embarrassed that she had caused a commotion. Now how would she explain the dumb backwards words to Miss Jones?

Miss Jones looked Katie straight in the eye.

"What happened?" the teacher asked.

Katie was determined not to cry. She told her story, even showing Miss Jones the 3x5 index card with the words Villa Park hand-printed on it.

"I read the words Villa Park backwards and it made me laugh out loud," Katie said, looking down at the floor so she did not have to look at her teacher.

"You read it backwards?" Miss Jones said. She had never heard that one before.

The teacher looked at the card and tried to read the words backwards.

She saw that Villa Park backwards was Krap Alliv. The teacher figured it out.

Miss Jones did not smile or laugh. She waited a moment before she said anything. She did not want to seem amused during a serious talk.

"It's always good when you practice your reading, even if you are reading words backwards and then trying to pronounce the nonsense words." Miss Jones said. "But when we talk about local history, you need to focus on local history.

"You have to pay attention," the teacher said. "You can't be disruptive."

Katie kept looking down. She expected to be punished for causing a commotion.

Laguna Beach is known as The OC's Art Colony

"Katie, I expect that you will do a very good job in finding a secret about Villa Park," Miss Jones said, adding sharply, "and your secret cannot involve saying the city's name backwards."

Katie looked up for the first time. She was still embarrassed, but she was feeling a little better. She knew Miss Jones was fair. She would be punished, but it would be fair.

116

"Because you disrupted the class, I'm going to give you a time-out for the rest of this recess," Miss Jones said. "I'm glad you practice your reading, but we cannot have outbursts in class."

Katie went outside and sat alone on the hard bench for a few minutes. She thought about what she did. Villa Park backwards did not seem so funny.

When the class came in, Katie went to her regular seat. No one said anything to her. No one asked why she laughed out loud.

When Miss Jones talked about Orange County's being a part of the Old West, Katie listened carefully. Miss Jones said Anaheim, and then Santa Ana, were the end of the line for the big railroads. The railroads brought real change to Orange County.

OC Archives
*Silent film star Buster Keaton clowns in front of an 1881 locomotive.*

Railroads brought in new farmers and new families looking for fresh starts. Religious groups flourished. A colony of talented Polish writers and actors, including the famous stage actress, Helena Modjeska, moved to Anaheim.

Trains also brought in gunslingers and criminals. One Tustin lawman

117

said that in the 1870s and 1880s, every man carried a gun. He said wearing a big six-shooter on your hip was as common as wearing a big cowboy hat on your head.

In those Old West days, Miss Jones said, Santa Ana was known for its saloons and its tough customers.

Anaheim Public Library

*In 1908, Anaheim bartender William F. Stark's (center) Exchange Saloon was an Old West saloon in an old-time town. Stark was later elected mayor of Anaheim.*

**Desperados** would ride their horses through Anaheim every day. Orange County was a rough place.

Miss Jones said the Orange County Board of Supervisors tried to **civilize** the county. They passed laws forbidding rowdy cowboys from riding their horses into businesses or saloons. The supervisors also banned horses from walking on wood-plank sidewalks, a law that angered unruly **ruffians** in Huntington Beach.

The cowboys **protested** the horse-on-sidewalk ban, even posing for a photograph with their horses' rear hooves defiantly placed on the wood-planked sidewalk as a way to mock the supervisors.

*Cowboys protesting the horse-on-sidewalk ban in Huntington Beach*

The protests had little effect. Time was on the side of civilized behavior. The wide-open Old West days were fading into the past.

Over time, horse and buggy rigs were replaced by horseless carriages called cars. Dirt roads were paved. Voters passed laws closing saloons. Houses had electric lights and indoor plumbing.

Things changed.

In 1902, Buffalo Bill Cody reminded Orange County of the dangers of the untamed frontier when he brought his famous Wild West traveling show to Santa Ana.

FIRST LAST AND ONLY VISIT

# Santa Ana, One Day Only, FRIDAY, Sept. 26

## "AU REVOIR" RECEPTION

Another European Tour Arranged for This

**SUPERLATIVELY POPULAR HISTORICAL ENTERTAINMENT.**

# BUFFALO BILL'S WILD WEST
## AND ROUGH RIDERS OF THE WORLD.

**An Educational Exhibition**
That really means something.

**A Veritable Kindergarten of History**
Teaching facts and not on fiction founded.

**FEATURE PILED ON FEATURE**
This season surpassing its own stupendous self.

**MORE** Peerless Riders, Warlike Pageants, Chivalrous Characters, Strange People,
Than ever before presented.

**NEW** Nations and Nomads, Pictures of Border Life, Equestrian Feats and Skill, Scouts, Soldiers and Horses,
Fresh from field and foray.

**FEATURES** U. S. LIFE-SAVERS. ATLANTIC COAST GUARDS. Thrilling Rescues by the Breeches Buoy.
All under the personal command of "The King of Them All",

## COL. W. F. CODY, "BUFFALO BILL"
And NATE SALSBURY, Director-General.

**LIVING OBJECT LESSONS**
Taken from the pages of realism, and illustrated by the very men who have assisted in making the fame of the

**World's Mounted Warriors**
Together with those true born Pioneers of the Plains who have told the story of progress in the Great Drama of Civilization. New and interesting arrangement of well-known Wild West incidents, such as

**The Stage Coach "Hold Up", Cowboy "Round Up", and Attack on the Emigrant Train.**

# GRAND FREE STREET REVIEW
On the morning of Exhibition, exact hour and route of parade to be announced.
The *piece de resistance* being the vivid and

## THRILLING MILITARY SPECTACLE OF THE BATTLE OF SAN JUAN HILL.

Two Performances Daily 2 and 8 p. m., rain or shine, Admission 50c, Children under 9 years, 25c. Reserved Seats (including admission) $1.00, on sale at Bristol & Rowley's drug store Fourth and Main Sts

Buffalo Bill paraded Indians in full war paint through Santa Ana streets, and then put on a dazzling show that included daring Pony Express stunt riding, Annie Oakley's fancy trick shots, and a fake shoot-out between brave cowboys and scary Indians.

However, Buffalo Bill's vivid re-creation of Old West dangers did not discourage families from braving frontier hardships and crossing the Great Plains to reach civilized places like Orange County.

Miss Jones said the new families moving to Orange County were looking for safety and security, not the violent Old West portrayed in Buffalo Bill's traveling show.

Katie was expressionless as Miss Jones talked about the OC and the Old West.

*After an 1893 rabbit-hunting party, Anaheim men and boys display the long-legged and long-eared jackrabbits they bagged with long rifles.*

She was interested in Buffalo Bill and Orange County becoming more civilized, but she was not going to do anything to cause a commotion. She was just going to sit and listen. There would be no more outbursts from her.

Katie doodled as she listened to the teacher. She really couldn't help herself. She wrote Llib Ola Ffub on her notebook.

Llib Ola Ffub was Buffalo Bill backwards.

Katie's mouth turned up just a tiny bit as she wrote it.

Llib Ola Ffub.

She had to smile.

A Slice in Time

*Real estate tycoon David Hewes' El Modena packinghouse opened in 1898.*

**Ellen F. Smith**
(1838-1922)

In 1911, a 72-year-old Socialist named Ellen F. Smith became the first Orange County woman to register to vote.

She was standing outside the County Clerk's office early in the morning of October 14, 1911, waiting for the doors to open so she could be the first female to register to vote in Orange County.

The Santa Ana woman said she wanted to vote against saloons and to end the evil of alcohol.

Ellen Smith was allowed to vote after California voters—all men—voted in 1911 to let women cast ballots in state and local elections.

California women still could not vote in federal elections until the 19th amendment to the U.S. Constitution became law nine years later, in 1920.

In 2010, more women than men were registered to vote in Orange County.

# 15 OLD SHERIFFS, A CRACK SHOT

Katie decided to do her backwards trick as Miss Jones handed back a math quiz.

When Miss Jones passed the quizzes back, Katie looked at other people's papers and pronounced their names backwards. Lindsey became Yes d nil. Amber became Reb ma. Nikki was Ikkin. Alex became Xela.

"Xela—excellent," said Katie, lowering her chin, drumming her fingertips together and doing a halfway good imitation of Mr. Burns's voice on the cartoon show *The Simpsons.* Everyone giggled.

When Katie saw Lee Berry's math quiz, she said his backwards name was Yrreb Eel. If Lee remembered the time she called him Eel, he did not say anything. He just laughed. Katie smiled and enjoyed being the center of attention.

After a little more giggling over backwards names, Miss Jones told everyone to settle down and to think some more about the Old West and the days when Orange County was filled with dusty frontier towns and dangerous gunslingers.

Miss Jones said the first man elected to enforce the law in Old West Orange County was a Westminster general-store owner named Richard Harris. Dick Harris was elected Orange County's first sheriff in 1889.

Sheriff Harris was a handsome man with a big bushy mustache. He was a **strict** sheriff who believed in law and order. He carried a gun. He enforced the law. He arrested bad guys and put them in the county jail.

However, Miss Jones said, the sheriff did not like to carry his pistol in a holster. He kept his six-shooter in his pants' rear pocket, pointed down, with the gun handle sticking out.

Sandra Hutchens is Orange County's first female sheriff

One day, as Sheriff Harris pulled his pistol out of his pocket, he got his gun caught in his pants and it went off by mistake. Miss Jones said the sheriff shot himself in the rear end.

Chris could not believe what he was hearing.

The sheriff shot himself in the butt?

Yes. Sheriff Harris really shot himself in the rear end, but it was only a flesh wound. The sheriff recovered, but his pride—and his reputation—were wounded.

Voters lost confidence in Sheriff Harris after the shooting accident. He wasn't re-elected. Theo Lacy was elected to wear the sheriff's badge in 1890.

Miss Jones said Sheriff Lacy was a much more successful lawman than Dick Harris. Theo Lacy was the sheriff for many years, and he helped build a solid, escape-proof county jail in Santa Ana, a jail that was called Lacy's Hotel.

In 1901, the red-sandstone County Courthouse, the county government's most famous building, opened next to the jail. More than 100 years later, long after Lacy's Hotel was gone, the Old County Courthouse was still being used in downtown Santa Ana.

First American

*Sheriff Theo Lacy*

Katie had seen the Old Courthouse from the window of her mom's minivan. It was surrounded by big trees and big buildings. It had a nice lawn with a couple of cannons out front, but the Old Courthouse looked a little old-fashioned and a little out of place.

Still, Katie liked that the Old Courthouse was still being used. What did Miss Jones say? History is alive all around us. The Old Courthouse was a part of Orange County's living history.

*The still-standing old county courthouse shown in a 1901 photograph.*

Talking about the Old Courthouse was fine, Katie thought, but she was getting impatient. She did not want to talk about old buildings or a sheriff who shot himself in the butt.

She needed to talk with Miss Jones. She needed to know if the Villa Park secrets she found were good enough to give her a special spot in the Secret Club.

When the class went outside, Katie's friends wanted her to do her backwards trick again, but she needed to talk to Miss Jones. She stalled around a moment or two and then walked up to the teacher.

Katie said she knew a secret about Villa Park. Her mom had helped her find it. Miss Jones listened politely.

Katie said Villa Park was the only Orange County city with no churches. Not a single church in the entire city. Was that a good secret?

"No," said Miss Jones with a sympathetic smile.

"That is a fun fact about the city," she said. "You're right when you say there are no churches in Villa Park. And there is no park in Villa Park, either, but those are fun facts, not secrets."

Katie was disappointed. Her mom had taken her to Villa Park's tiny library to find a secret about Villa Park. Now Miss Jones was telling her that her secret wasn't a secret.

Katie felt bad, but she was determined not to cry.

Miss Jones could see Katie was trying very hard to do something extra so she could earn a special spot in the Secret Club. The teacher helped her out.

"Katie, we don't pronounce your city's name '*VEE-yah Park*' like the Mexican bandit Pancho Villa. We say '*VIL-lah Park*' with two hard Ls," Miss Jones said. "Why is that?"

Katie perked up. The answer, she thought, must be a secret. The city's name must be a riddle or something. If she solved the mystery of Villa Park's name, she would have a real secret and she could get a special spot in the Secret Club.

While Katie was thinking about her city's name, Chris was ready to talk about his secret. He was going to talk about the City of Stanton and the mystery of a ghost town called Orangethorpe.

And he was going to talk about bathrooms.

Not just bathrooms, he thought. Indoor plumbing.

Chris cracked a crazy smile.

Indoor plumbing would be his key to the Secret Club.

A Slice in Time

*Cowboys roping giant oranges was a 1920s image in Tustin.*

**Nelson M. Holderman**
**(1885-1953)**

Nelson M. Holderman was Orange County's first great military hero.

A Tustin walnut grower and a county road crew worker, he was a leader of World War I's Lost Battalion.

In 1918, Holderman and his troops were trapped behind enemy lines in France's Argonne Forest, surrounded and outnumbered by enemy soldiers using flame-throwers and machine guns. In fierce hand-to-hand fighting, Holderman was wounded repeatedly but he would not give up.

After five days of bloody battles, Holderman and his men were saved. His courage under fire made him one of the world's most famous soldiers. He received the Congressional Medal of Honor, America's highest military award, for his bravery.

After the war, he commanded the Yountville Soldier's Home, a facility now called the Nelson Holderman Hospital. Tustin's Holderman Park is named for his famous family.

HOLDERMAN PARK

# 16 Vanishing Cities

Chris needed help with his homework. A lot of help. He hated homework.

Chris's mom helped him by looking up the City of Stanton's website. Using the Internet, she found some puzzling stuff.

The website said the City of Stanton was named after Philip A. Stanton, an influential Speaker of the California Assembly. Phil Stanton also founded two other coastal towns, Bay City and Pacific City.

Chris's mom said she had never heard of Phil Stanton or Bay City or Pacific City.

And she was confused about how a town called Stanton could become an Orange County city in 1911 and then become an Orange County city again in 1956.

"Weird," said Chris.

Chris's mom said Stanton had two different birthdays— May 15, 1911, and May 23, 1956.

"Weird," Chris said. He was saying "weird" a lot. Strange things happened in the past.

To solve the mysteries, Chris's mom did a little more Internet research.

*Seal Beach's oceanfront Joy Zone in about 1925.*

It turned out that Bay City and Pacific City each changed their names more than 100 years ago. She said that Bay City changed its name to Seal Beach, and Pacific City became Huntington Beach.

"Cities changed their names?" Chris said.

Chris's mom said she knew about other Orange County cities that had changed their names too.

She said the City of Cypress was once called Dairy Valley and the City of La Palma was once called Dairyland. Those cities changed their names when families and schools moved in and cows and dairies moved out.

"Dairyland," said Chris. "It sounds like Disneyland for cows."

Chris's mom told him to focus on Stanton, not a Disneyland for cows.

Chris did not say anything, but he was thinking about a Disneyland for cows. Cows spinning in teacups. Cows stuffed in little Autopia cars. Cows getting soaked as they floated down Grizzly Rapids.

While Chris was daydreaming about cows on Splash Mountain with their front hooves held high, his mom was looking at the computer screen, trying to figure out why the City of Stanton had two birthdays.

As she searched, Chris's mom began talking about indoor plumbing, water pipes, and toilets. This was getting weird, Chris thought.

Chris's mom said that in the early 1900s, modern houses were being built with indoor plumbing for the first time. Indoor plumbing meant big changes in people's lives.

Rather than carrying buckets of water into homes, water came in through pipes. Rather than having smelly outhouses in the backyard, modern homes had indoor flush toilets.

The new indoor plumbing was very **convenient**, but it created new problems for cities. How did water get to houses? What happened when water went down the drain or when someone flushed a toilet? Where would the wastewater and **sewage** go?

First American

*A contented cow pulls a milk wagon from Buena Park's Lily Creamery.*

In Anaheim, it poured into a big pipe buried beneath city streets. Anaheim planned to empty the pipes by dumping the stinky raw sewage into an open field where it could dry in the sun or seep into the soil.

When the City of Anaheim bought farmer John Gilbert's ranch for its planned sewer farm, nearby farmers went crazy.

The farmers did not want Anaheim's sewer farm's stinky smells near their homes. They complained about health risks. They held protest meetings. They yelled at Anaheim politicians.

The *Orange County Register* was founded in 1905

No one listened to them. Anaheim pushed ahead with its plans.

The farmers were mad and unhappy until prominent politician Philip Stanton, who owned property near the Gilbert Ranch, came up with a clever plan.

Stanton told the farmers to form their own city. He said a new city could forbid sewer farms inside the new city's boundaries. A new city could stop Anaheim's smelly plans.

The farmers formed a big city—at more than 10 square miles it was the biggest city in 1911 Orange County—and the new city banned sewer farms.

Phil Stanton's plan worked perfectly. The farmers stopped the stinky sewer farm. They named their new city after sewer farm fighter Phil Stanton.

After the City of Stanton was formed, some farmers started complaining loudly about city taxes being too high. Many said that once the sewer farm fight was over, they did not need a city government. They wanted lower taxes, not more government.

*In 1913, the Stanton Improvement Company sold new homes and new farms in the new city.*

While the Stanton farmers **griped**, other farmers living west of Fullerton got wind of the City of Fullerton's 1921 plans to buy a ranch they could use as a sewer farm.

The West Fullerton farmers decided to copy Stanton's **strategy** and form a new city to block Fullerton's sewer farm plans. The farmers called their new city the City of Orangethorpe.

"The City of Orangethorpe?" Chris's mom said out loud.

138

She had never heard of a City of Orangethorpe. It was not on the Orange County map. It was not on the list of Orange County cities. Orangethorpe was a big street, not a city.

As an Orange County city, it simply did not exist.

Orangethorpe was a **phantom** city.

Chris's mom looked at him. She was tired.

"It's getting late," she said. "We'll work on this later."

Chris's mom clicked out of Google, got up and began picking up tree branches and sticks on her kitchen floor. The stuff on the floor was part of the Excellent Stick Collection created by Chris's little brother, Matthew. Matthew was already asleep on the couch.

Chris was not paying much attention to his mom or his sleeping brother. He was imagining cows at Disneyland riding in the Main Street parade, waving hoofs at cheering crowds.

Weird, he thought.

But cows at Disneyland made as much sense to him as cities not knowing their birthdays. Or big political fights over smelly sewer farms. Or ghost towns that vanished.

It was all just weird.

*A white top hat and a burning firecracker highlight this 1932 Western Lithograph-produced label.*

**Philip A. Stanton**
**(1868-1945)**

The 37th Speaker of the California Assembly, Philip Axley Stanton was a big Orange County builder.

He helped develop today's cities of Huntington Beach, Seal Beach and Stanton and helped create Seal Beach's "Joy Zone," a long-gone, beachfront amusement park famed for its all-wood roller coaster.

An unsuccessful candidate for the 1910 Republican nomination for Governor, Philip Stanton served four terms in the State Assembly, representing Los Angeles's 71st District. In the 1930s, he served on the California Highway Commission.

Today, Philip Stanton's hacienda-style Anaheim home is a part of the Fairmont Preparatory Academy's Anaheim campus.

The City of Stanton, as well as Stanton Avenue, is named in his honor.

# 17 ORANGES, The King of Crops

Chris was not sure if he knew enough to get a special spot in the Secret Club.

He had some good stuff. He knew the City of Stanton was named after a guy named Philip Stanton, a big-time politician who helped some farmers stop a smelly sewer farm scheme almost 100 years ago.

He thought that sounded good, but Chris worried that his Stanton secrets were a little too easy to find. He was not sure if he had a real secret.

He knew he had loose ends to tie up, too. Like why Stanton had two birthdays. Like why cities changed their names. And like why the City of Orangethorpe vanished.

Chris could not answer those questions. Neither could his mom.

So Chris decided to talk to Miss Jones. He always felt shy about asking the teacher one-to-one questions. He did not know why; he just felt uncomfortable.

But Chris wanted to earn a special spot in the Secret Club, so he was going to talk with his teacher.

First, he would wait for just the right time, a time late in the day. Then, when school was over, he would ask her if what he knew was good enough to get him a special spot in the Secret Club.

He just had to wait and fidget while Miss Jones talked about packinghouses and orange groves and water for agriculture.

First American

*Orange crates roll along a packinghouse conveyor belt.*

Miss Jones said big-time farming began to replace cattle-ranching and sheep-grazing about the time that the railroads began using refrigerated freight cars to keep farm products fresh on the long train trips to other parts of the nation.

The farmers were able to grow more crops by using electric power to pump **irrigation water** to their farms and citrus groves. Irrigation water brought the land to life.

With a reliable source of water, farmers turned the county's sheep- and cattle-grazing pastures into a world-class farming region, a place that was perfect for growing citrus—oranges, lemons and grapefruits—and other money-making crops like lima beans, sugar beets, chili peppers and celery.

*Wagonloads of Westminster sugar beets wait to be loaded on eastbound trains.*

Orange County farmers grew many fine products, but the Valencia Orange was the King of Crops.

Orange County's first commercial Valencia orange groves were planted on land that is now California State University, Fullerton.

A Fullerton businessman named Charles C. Chapman made a fortune by figuring out how to sell his fresh, flavorful Valencia oranges nationally. Other citrus ranchers, who could not harvest as many sweet-tasting oranges as Charles Chapman, followed his example by banding together to sell their citrus crops nationally.

The ranchers organized around packinghouses, the large warehouses where oranges were sorted, washed, packed into crates, loaded on to railroad cars and distributed nationally. By working together, the ranchers were able to get top dollar for their tasty citrus products.

The largest and most **influential** citrus distributor was a packinghouse partnership called the Southern California Fruit Exchange, an association of orange grove owners known by the famous Sunkist brand.

The Sunkist partnership was nationally influential, but in Orange County nothing matched the Irvine Ranch's influence as an agricultural powerhouse.

When ranch owner James H. Irvine, the son of ranch founder James Irvine, solved his water problems, he was able to develop one of the world's greatest farming operations.

Citrus **flourished** on the Irvine Ranch. Other crops, including sugar beets, black-eyed peas, and lima beans, also thrived. Beans were especially successful. At one time, C.J. Segerstrom's Costa Mesa lima bean field was the largest in the nation. Some said the Irvine Ranch was the biggest bean field in the world.

*Carl J. Segerstrom*

*A photo promoting the 1921 Anaheim Orange Show.*

With the Irvine Ranch leading the way, Orange County was one of America's great farmlands for more than 50 years.

After Miss Jones finished talking about oranges and agriculture, Chris waited around to talk to her. After class, he told her about indoor plumbing and the Anaheim sewer farms and a guy named Philip Stanton.

"That's pretty good," Miss Jones said, nodding her approval. "What else did you learn?"

He blurted out that some cities changed their names. And Stanton had two birthdays. And there was a mysterious city called Orangethorpe that fit in somewhere.

Miss Jones had a small smile. She knew something.

"You're very close to finding a real local history secret," she said. "Keep looking."

She paused, and then added, "Here are two hints. First, Orangethorpe is a forgotten town, a real city that disappeared. And, second, learn about the word ***disincorporation***. That word will help solve your mysteries."

Weird, Chris thought. He wondered how a word he had never heard before—disincorporation—could be the key to unlocking the mystery.

He paused for a moment. The only way this could get any weirder, he thought, would be if that Know-It-All Katie tried to say disincorporation backwards in some **gobbledygook** language.

What a weirdo, Chris thought. A *weirdo sourpuss Know-It-All.*

Commercial artist J. Duncan Gleason's wife Dorothy was the model for Sonia.

**James H. Irvine**
(1867-1947)

James Harvey Irvine—known as "J.I."—inherited the Irvine Ranch in 1892 when he was 25 years old.

For the next 55 years, he transformed his land from a cattle- and sheep-grazing ranch into one of the greatest agricultural operations in the world.

When he **incorporated** the Irvine Company in 1894, it was one of California's first corporations.

An outdoorsman, he loved having his pack of hunting dogs around—even inside his Irvine Ranch home and, occasionally, at big business meetings.

In 1937, he formed the James Irvine Foundation, a billion dollar charity that supports the arts, education and community development.

In 1897, he gave Orange County its first regional park. The City of Irvine, as well as streets, schools, and parks, are named for James Irvine and the Irvine family.

# 18 The Super Special MEMBER

Chris handed his mom a scrap of paper with the word "disincorporation" written on it in cursive handwriting.

He said Miss Jones wrote the word down for him and told him that it was the key to unlocking the secrets of Stanton and Orangethorpe.

Chris's mom looked at the strange word, then said, "Let's Google this."

She sat down at the computer and typed in the words "disincorporation" "Stanton" and "Orangethorpe."

Chris's mom wanted to solve the local history mystery even more than Chris. She studied the web hits that popped up. After a few moments, she looked at Chris.

"I think I get this," Chris's mom said. "People in Stanton and Orangethorpe voted to become cities to stop other cities from putting sewer farms in their neighborhoods. Voting to form a city is called *incorporation*.

"But once the threat of the sewer farms was gone, the people who lived in those two cities did not want to pay high city taxes," she said. "So they held new elections and voted to *disincorporate*—or quit being cities."

Orangethorpe quit being a city in 1923, and Stanton quit in 1924. Both disincorporated areas had lower taxes and no city councils. They became a part of county territory, once again under the board of supervisors' **jurisdiction**.

Over time, the old City of Orangethorpe became parts of Fullerton or Anaheim or Buena Park. Much of the old City of Stanton became a part of Anaheim or Buena Park or Garden Grove.

Then the whole disincorporation thing started getting complicated. And, of course, it started getting weird.

OC Archives

*In 1956, new housing tracts were springing up throughout the re-incorporated City of Stanton.*

"The strange thing is that some people in the old City of Stanton did not want to become a part of another city," Chris's mom said. "So they campaigned to become a city again, 32 years after they voted to stop being a city.

"Because Stanton incorporated, then disincorporated, then incorporated again, it has two birthdays—the one in 1911 when Stanton incorporated the first time, and the one in 1956 when Stanton incorporated a second time."

*Today's Stanton Civic Center*

Not good, Chris thought. This was going to be hard to explain. It would be even harder to write down.

Chris's mom said she would help him make sense of his secret. And she would help him with his report on the mysteries of Stanton and Orangethorpe.

Chris was not happy about writing his report. This was hard stuff. He started writing, but he had to show his mom almost every sentence he wrote. She made suggestions. He made changes. He used a lot of paper. This was hard.

He wanted to go outside and play, but he stayed with it.

It took a long time for Chris to write his secrets down on paper, but when it was done, he thought it was pretty good. So did his mom.

The next day, Chris gave his report to Miss Jones. She thanked him.

Later, Miss Jones was holding Chris's paper in her hand when she talked about local history mysteries.

"Christopher is the first person to solve a local history mystery and to become a Super Special Member of the Secret Club," Miss Jones said. "He went beyond finding a few Fun Facts. He found—and solved—a real mystery about cities that vanished."

To explain, the teacher talked about indoor plumbing and how Phillip Stanton suggested forming a new city to fight Anaheim's sewer farm plan, then how Orangethorpe was created for the same reason.

When the sewer farm threat was gone, Miss Jones talked about disincorporation and how voters wiped the City of Orangethorpe off the map for all time. She told how Stanton made a 1956 comeback as a city.

She said Anaheim, Fullerton and other cities also found a way to solve their sewer problems without building smelly sewer farms.

Miss Jones said cities banded together to build a big system of sewage pipes from inland Orange County

First American

*A team of mules helps dig a ditch for sewer pipes.*

to the ocean—a sewer to the sea. The sewer to the sea went far out in the ocean, taking raw sewage deep into the ocean and eliminating the need for sewer farms.

Over time, the 1920s-era pipelines became a part of today's Orange County Sanitation District and its Fountain Valley sewage treatment plant.

Chris did not hear a word Miss Jones was saying. His mind was racing.

He was thinking about being the first Super Special Member of the Secret Club. He was proud. He liked doing well. His mom had helped him, but he had worked really hard, too. He felt really, really good.

He even liked history a little bit. Just a *little* bit.

Chris heard Miss Jones mention his name again. He zeroed in on what she was saying.

"Christopher has told us about two full-fledged cities that disincorporated," she said. "Stanton and Orangethorpe quit being cities. One disappeared forever.

"But besides the forgotten City of Orangethorpe, there are other Orange County ghost towns—mysterious little towns that vanished or were absorbed by other cities or who changed their names."

She smiled her little smile. She knew things she was not telling.

"Like Christopher, see if you can find out something about these little ghost towns. Look at the past of the city on your card," she said. "Tell us about your city's secret past.

"If you can solve a local history mystery, you can join Chris as a Super Special Member of the Secret Club."

*The Orangethorpe Citrus Association packed fruit from 1923 to 1950.*

**Col. S.H. Finley**
**(1863-1944)**

Solomon Henderson Finley was Orange County's first great civil engineer.

A U.S. Army veteran, Colonel Finley engineered the county's first paved road network, helped craft the first sewer to the sea, built the county's first concrete dam and designed water systems in five Orange County cities.

A Democratic politician as well as a civil engineer, he was elected mayor of Santa Ana, county surveyor and, for three terms, Orange County Supervisor.

In 1928, Col. Finley was chosen as the first-ever secretary of the regional Metropolitan Water District (MWD). He was an MWD officer for 13 years, helping build great **aqueducts** to bring Colorado River water to Southern California.

Finley Avenue, next to the Newport Beach City Hall on Balboa Peninsula, is named for him.

# 19 Spanglish

The day after Chris became a Super Special Member of the Secret Club, Miss Jones was flooded with local history stories and secrets.

Everyone wanted to be a Super Special Member of the Secret Club.

One of the kids in the class, a boy named Jacob, said that real estate promoters renamed Pacific City to Huntington Beach because they wanted real estate mogul Henry E. Huntington to run his Red Car **trolleys** into the seaside community. The **flattery** worked.

OC Archives

*With the Huntington Beach Pier in the background,*
*workers build a trolley line to Newport Beach.*

Pacific City was renamed Huntington Beach and the town got its trolley line. Over time, workers extended the trolley line to Newport Beach.

Others told their teacher about Orange County's forgotten towns. A boy named R.J.—his real name was Ryan James, but everyone called him R.J.—talked about settlements like Olive and McPherson that became a part of the City of Orange.

Some towns changed their names more than once. A blonde boy named Aiden talked about Aliso City becoming a town called El Toro and then, after a pretty big political fight over the town's name, El Toro incorporated as the City of Lake Forest in 1991.

Lee Berry said that the City of Westminster was called Tri-City when it incorporated in 1957. The name Tri-City was picked because community leaders wanted to combine three little towns—Westminster, Barber City and Midway City—into one big city.

At the last minute, Midway City dropped out of the deal. Westminster and Barber City voted to incorporate anyway, but the name Tri-City no longer made any sense. So, less than a year after it became a city, Tri-City changed its name to Westminster.

So, over time, Tri-City was wiped off the map. Barber City was forgotten. Westminster was named a 1996 All-America City. Westminster officials proudly placed "All-America City" signs around their town.

The little unincorporated town of Midway City also still exists, Lee said. It is on Beach Boulevard, just north of the San Diego Freeway.

"Good job, Eel," said Katie after Lee finished his report. Lee smiled.

Katie listened politely as her classmates talked about cities changing names, old towns becoming parts of bigger cities, and ghost towns that simply disappeared.

She was interested when a smart boy named Cooper talked about old trolley stops on three long-forgotten Pacific Electric Railway lines. Some of the old Red Car trolley stops had funny names, like *Buaro*, a Spanish word for "buzzard."

Katie was interested in places with Spanish names. She knew Mission Viejo meant old mission in Spanish and Costa Mesa was Spanish for coastal plain.

Many Orange County streets had Spanish names. Camino de Estrella meant highway of the star in Spanish. La Palma (Spanish for the palm) was the name of a little city and a big street.

*Mission Viejo means old mission in Spanish.*

Alana Cacciatori

But Katie was sure her City of Villa Park did not have a Spanish name nor a name that was that odd mix of English and Spanish words that was sometimes called **Spanglish**.

Buena Park—good park—was a city with a Spanglish name: It was a mix of Spanish (*Buena*) and English (Park). Oso Parkway—bear parkway—was Spanglish. So was *Trabuco* Canyon Road: Trabuco was the Spanish word for blunderbuss, an old-fashioned shotgun. *Canyon* and *Road* were English words.

Cool word, *blunderbuss*, thought Katie, her mind slowly drifting off.

Katie quickly refocused. She had to stay **disciplined**. She could not be distracted by cool words. She had to focus.

She was sure that Villa Park was not a Spanglish name, and it was not a part of Orange County's rich Spanish and Mexican **heritage**.

Alana Cacciatori

Katie had found a paperback book by Orange County historian Phil Brigandi that said, "the name Villa Park was probably meant to suggest refined country living. The name has always been pronounced like the English *vil-luh*, not the Spanish *vee-yah*."

English, not Spanish.

Even though Villa Park had different names in the past—known as Mountain View for a while and once called Wanda—Katie knew Villa Park was where you found villas—with two hard Ls. It was a little city with big houses and big yards.

Katie included her Villa Park Fun Facts about the city not having a park or a church and the quote from

Mr. Brigandi. Her report was a part of the flood of papers that hit Miss Jones' desk after Chris became a Super Special Member of the Secret Club.

Later that day, after hearing a few reports on local mysteries, Miss Jones stood up, holding Katie's paper. She said she was going to give Katie's Villa Park report.

Katie was surprised. Miss Jones had not talked about anyone else's report.

This was **unusual**.

Katie did not know what would happen next.

El Pavo Real *means The Peacock in Spanish.*

**Gonzalo Mendez**
**(1912-1964)**

In 1945, five Mexican-American families filed a federal lawsuit saying their children were not getting a good education in Orange County schools. They said schools were illegally **segregating** Mexican-Americans from white students.

The five fathers—Tomas Estrada, William Guzman, Gonzalo Mendez, Frank Palomino and Lorenzo Ramirez—said their children were forced to go to bad schools with poorly paid teachers and old schoolbooks. The five fathers said it was unfair. Their lawsuit was called *Mendez vs. Westminster*.

The five fathers won their lawsuit, leading to a 1947 state law saying all children—Asian, Black, White or Latino—should get the same education.

The landmark *Mendez vs. Westminster* court case was honored with a U.S. Postage stamp in 2007. Gonzalo and Felicitas Mendez Intermediate School in Santa Ana is named for the Orange County civil rights pioneers.

# 20 Our Shared Past

When Miss Jones looked at the papers in her hand, her glasses slid down her nose.

Miss Jones pushed her glasses up and said Katie wrote a fine report on Villa Park. The teacher said Katie explored Villa Park's past to learn about the city's name.

On the surface, Miss Jones said, almost everyone would think a city in Orange County—a county that celebrates its Spanish and Mexican heritage in city and street names—would use the Spanish pronunciation *"VEE-yah"* in the City of Villa Park's name.

"Not so," said Miss Jones.

The City of Orange totally surrounds the City of Villa Park

She said Katie looked into the origins of the city's name and found **evidence** proving that villas—with two hard Ls—were big houses on big lots. Villa Park was full of big houses on big lots.

Miss Jones said that by looking at the English origin of Villa Park's name, Katie solved the mystery of why and how you pronounce the city's name.

"Actually, it isn't very important if a city or a street or a person has a Spanish name or an English name. Both languages have beautiful words that are a part of our shared history," Miss Jones said. "What is important is showing respect and saying things properly.

Joe Oftelie

*A center of tiny Villa Park is Villa Park High School, home of the Spartans.*

"It may seem like a small thing for you to try to pronounce English or Spanish names correctly," Miss Jones said, "but small things can make a big difference to people.

"Saying VIL-luh Park respect's the city's heritage," she said. "Saying VEE-yah Park is disrespectful, just like mispronouncing Spanish words or Spanish names is disrespectful.

"You can make a big difference by showing people a little respect."

Miss Jones looked at Katie and smiled.

"Katie took a little extra time and found out that Villa Park's name had an English origin, not a Spanish origin," she said. "In a county where so many places have beautiful Spanish names, she did a great job of finding out the real history of her city's name.

"Her extra effort was—"

Miss Jones put her hands together in front of her face, and began drumming her fingertips together, lowering her chin and talking like Mr. Burns on *The Simpsons.*

"—EX-cellent."

Katie and the class laughed. Miss Jones did not tell many jokes, so it was especially funny. Katie liked it because Miss Jones seemed to be copying her Mr. Burns imitation.

When all the laughing stopped, Miss Jones had one more surprise left. A serious surprise.

For solving the mystery of Villa Park's English name, Miss Jones said Katie was the second Super Special Member of the Secret Club.

Olympian oarsman Jim Workman was Villa Park Mayor nine times

Katie's face got a little red. She was excited and happy and a little embarrassed.

Lee told her that she did a good job. Her friends, even smart girls like Alana and Lauren, smiled at her. They made her feel good. She felt great.

After class, Chris walked up to Katie with his biggest, goofiest grin. Katie thought he was going to talk about the Secret Club.

Instead, Chris planned to try out a new joke. He thought it was a really good joke.

"I can hardly wait until tomorrow," Chris said.

"Why?" asked a confused Katie.

"Because," said Chris, smiling his goofy grin, "I get better looking every day."

Katie couldn't believe it. What a dumb thing to say, she thought. What a jerk.

"What-ever," she said. She did not smile. She turned and walked away.

"Awk-ward," said Chris in a funny voice, covering up his embarrassment.

Chris was surprised that Katie did not laugh at the joke. He thought it was funny. Maybe she didn't get it. Then Chris flashed on another idea.

Maybe the joke *wasn't* funny.

No. That couldn't be it, he thought. More likely, Katie was just a big grump who didn't get his awesome jokes.

He thought about it a while.

"She's just a sourpuss," Chris thought.

*A big sourpuss.*

*The pioneer Yorba family used the Esperanza citrus brand.*

**Gaddi H. Vasquez**
**(1955-present)**

A former Orange County Supervisor and City of Orange police officer, Gaddi Vasquez was the first member of his family to go to college and the first Hispanic to head the United States Peace Corps.

Beginning in 2002, he expanded the Peace Corps' international efforts to help rural countries, even sending Peace Corps volunteers to Mexico.

The Orange High graduate became Ambassador Vasquez in 2006 when former President George W. Bush named him as the United States' representative to the United Nations Agencies in Rome, Italy.

As a United States Ambassador, Gaddi Vasquez fought world hunger across the globe. He worked hard to bring food to starving children everywhere.

A gifted public speaker (in both English and Spanish), he now is a senior vice president for Southern California Edison Company.

# 21 WEIRD THINGS HAPPENED in the Past

Katie was sitting on her bed, thumbing through a thick paperback joke book, looking for something funny. The joke book wasn't very funny.

Most of the jokes were dumb, even dumber than Chris's lame jokes.

Here's one: What do you get when you cross a cuddly teddy bear with a Holstein cow?

Winnie the Mooh.

Weak, Katie thought. Cute, but weak. And not nearly good. She wanted to find something really, really funny.

When she found just the right joke, she would let that pain-in-the-pants Chris know what a really funny joke sounded like.

So far, she hadn't found the right joke. So she was going to keep on looking.

Later that day, Katie was still thinking about how to find jokes when Miss Jones began talking about Black Gold and how two big natural **disasters** shaped Orange County.

The teacher said that oil was Orange County's Black Gold. Since the 1890s, oil companies drilled in the Puente Hills north of Fullerton and in the Coyote Hills between La Habra and Buena Park, trying to find underground pools of crude oil.

They found one of the nation's great oilfields in the hills of North Orange County.

In what is now the City of Brea, and in what was once the old-time oil town of Olinda, oilmen hit it big. Soon, Placentia and La Habra had oil wells gushing. Oil rigs popped up every where. **Petroleum** production was big business.

City of Huntington Beach

Next to oranges, oil became North Orange County's number one product.

Orange County's biggest oil strike, however, was not in North County. It was in Huntington Beach, the city now nicknamed "Surf City, USA."

*Sculptor Edmond Shumpert's 1976 bronze statue of a surfer is at Huntington City Beach on Pacific Coast Highway.*

In the 1920s, Black Gold turned Huntington Beach into Oil City.

After the first Huntington Beach oil gusher hit, the city's oceanfront bluffs were quickly lined with tall wooden oil derricks. Oil refineries were built, and the sleepy, seaside city with the state's longest concrete pier became one of the nation's biggest oilfields.

First American

*In the 1920s, hundreds of wooden oil derricks lined the Huntington Beach shoreline.*

The oil industry, with its colorful oil-field workers and well-paying jobs, was booming on March 10, 1933, when Orange County was rocked by a giant earthquake.

Miss Jones said the killer quake shattered window panes, toppled buildings and killed more than 120 people in Southern California, including a Garden Grove High School girl who died when a wall collapsed on her.

In the aftermath of what was called the Long Beach Earthquake, the Orange County Board of Supervisors adopted strict **building codes** and **zoning** laws to protect people from future earthquake damage.

The county zoning laws greatly increased the supervisors' power over the way people could use their land. It made the supervisors more powerful.

Five years later, supervisors' duties were increased again when they responded to another **tragedy**, a disaster that the March 4, 1938, *New York Times* called "the worst flood in California history."

First American

*Earthquake debris crushed a car on a Santa Ana street in 1933.*

On a rainy March night, after days of thunderstorms, the Santa Ana River overflowed its banks, sending walls of water raging through Santa Ana Canyon and beyond.

At one point, the Santa Ana River rose five feet in five minutes, unleashing waves of water that flooded homes, smashed buildings,and washed away farms. The flood killed more than 20 people, most of them poor Mexican families in Anaheim and Placentia.

*The 1938 flood overwhelms downtown Buena Park.*

The morning after the flood, some families were trapped on their rooftops. Cars were flipped over. The strong river current had swept dairy cows away from Riverside and stranded them in Placentia orange trees. Everything was covered in mud.

Chris perked up.

Cows in trees?

He thought weird things happened in the past. This proved it.

Miss Jones, however, wasn't just talking about cows in orange trees. She was talking about flood control and the Prado Dam.

*The Prado Dam now protects Orange County from floods.*

Because of the death and destruction caused by the 1938 flood, Orange County Supervisors promised to tame the Santa Ana River to protect people from murderous floods.

The Supervisors bought land to build a great dam in Riverside County, just over the Orange County line. Supervisors said the huge Santa Ana River dam would prevent future flooding and protect people. They were right.

Miss Jones said the big dam—called the Prado Dam— was completed in 1941 after the U.S. Army Corps of Engineers took over the huge flood control job the county started.

Miss Jones said Prado Dam has a big mural painted on the main dam wall, with a drawing of the Liberty Bell and the phrase *200 Years of Freedom 1776–1976* hand-painted in big red, white and blue letters and numbers.

Chris remembered riding in his dad's car on the Riverside Freeway (State Route 91) looking out his car window and seeing the red, white and blue painting on the dam. He remembered asking his dad what it was all about.

His dad said the mural was painted to celebrate America's **bicentennial** birthday back in 1976. If he knew the name of the big dam, he did not mention it.

Chris's dad also did not say that the Prado Dam was built to stop the killer Santa Ana River from overflowing its banks or to protect people from flood danger.

Chris wished he'd known those things the first time he drove by the Prado Dam. He would have told everyone the story of the big flood and the big dam.

As a Super Special Member of the Secret Club, he could talk about the Prado Dam's secret history. He knew the dam's name. He could talk about why the big dam with the patriotic message was built and how it protected Orange County from floods.

And he could talk about real cows in real trees.

This could be cool.

A Slice in Time

*Goblins are mythical, mischievous creatures like trolls or gnomes.*

Charles C. Chapman
(1853-1944)

Chapman University is named for Fullerton **philanthropist** and businessman Charles Clarke Chapman.

A real estate **tycoon** who invested in orange groves and oil wells, he was called the "King of the Valencia Oranges."

Charles Chapman was the long-time president of the California Sunday School Association, served as Chairman of the California YMCA, and in 1904 became the first mayor of Fullerton.

He was California's candidate for the Republican Vice-Presidential nomination in 1924, but withdrew his name from consideration a few days before the Republican National Convention.

In addition to Chapman University, Chapman Avenue in the cities of Fullerton and Placentia is named in his honor.

CHAPMAN UNIVERSITY

# 22 Spies and Ninjas and Blimps

Katie could not find a good joke.

Before she went to school, she found a joke-riddle from her book and decided to try it out on her mom.

"What word is always spelled wrong?" Katie asked.

"I don't know," said her mom while working in the kitchen. "What?"

"Wrong," Katie said.

"What's wrong?" asked her mom, looking up.

"Wrong," said Katie. "Wrong is a word that's always spelled wrong—w-r-o-n-g—wrong."

Katie's mom thought for a moment, and then said, "Oh, I get it."

Katie's mom wiped her hands on a towel without smiling. Not good, Katie thought. It wasn't a very funny joke.

Katie decided her wrong joke wouldn't get any belly laughs at school. It was weaker than the Winnie the Mooh joke.

Katie was still thinking about jokes when she got to school and Miss Jones began talking about World War II and the military's clear marks on Orange County.

"After America entered World War II at the end of 1941, Orange County became the home to training centers and military airfields," Miss Jones said. "Thousands of soldiers and sailors and pilots passed through the county's big military bases.

First American

*Enlisted men arrive at SAAAB for World War II training.*

"And," she said, "a few Orange County–trained spies learned the black arts of **espionage** at secret training camps, including one on Catalina Island."

Chris perked up. Espionage? Secret training camps? Black arts? Spies?

Cool.

Miss Jones said that most military men in Orange County were not learning spycraft. Most were being tested, trained and then **deployed** to the war in the Pacific.

She said the very large number of soldiers, sailors and Marines living at Orange County military bases during World War II almost doubled the county's population.

Just before World War II, in 1940, about 131,000 men, women and children were living in all of Orange County. By the end of the war, 125,000 *more* service men and women were stationed in Orange County— pushing the county's wartime population to more than 250,000 people.

First American

*Sharp new soldiers march out of the SAAAB base.*

The county's biggest World War II military base was the long-forgotten Santa Ana Army Air Base (SAAAB) in what is now Costa Mesa. More than 200,000 servicemen passed through SAAAB.

While the Santa Ana base was booming, thousands of Marines were flying out of the Marine Corps Air Station at El Toro. Others served at the unique Santa Ana Lighter-than-Air Station with its big blimp hangars. In 1941, the Army also took over the tiny Orange County Airport.

The USA fought in World War II from 1941 to 1945

Besides Army and Marine **aviators**, Miss Jones said the Navy also had an Orange County beachhead. Sailors worked at the Seal Beach Naval Weapons Depot. Navy flyers trained at the Los Alamitos Naval Air Station and at the Mile Square airfield.

She said there also were secret agents and spies slipping into South Orange County during the war years.

She said a San Clemente Beach Club was the west coast headquarters of the Office of Strategic Services (OSS), the super-secret government agency that later became the Central Intelligence Agency (CIA).

In the 1940s, Miss Jones said, many spies-in-training went from Orange County to a secret training camp on Catalina Island, where they learned how to live off the land, how to use dangerous explosives, how to fight with knives and other **survival** skills.

Chris thought spy training camps were cool. He began imagining furious fights between Catalina-trained American spies and fierce Japanese ninja warriors. It was almost like a video game in his imagination.

When Miss Jones said Orange County's greatest contribution to winning World War II was training pilots and aviators for the Army, Navy and Marines, Chris did not hear her. He was thinking about secret agents and ninjas.

Chris's brain was jolted back into his classroom when Miss Jones started talking about the ghosts of World War II military bases. Talk of ghosts always got Chris's attention.

"The military's **legacy**—the ghosts of their past—is all around us today," Miss Jones said. "The military bases became a major part of our civic lives.

189

"The Old Santa Ana Army Air Base is now the Orange County Fairgrounds, Orange Coast College, Vanguard University, the Pacific Amphitheatre, the Costa Mesa Civic Center and parks and homes and businesses," she said. "It is a vital part of our county."

More than fifty years after the Santa Ana Army Air Base was closed, Miss Jones said Orange County politicians fought a political war over the future of another closed military base, the El Toro Marine Corps Air Station.

When the U.S. Congress decided to close the El Toro base in 1999, the City of Newport Beach, the county and North County cities wanted to turn the old Marine Corps Air Station's runways into a big international airport.

El Toro MCAS's fate was voted on four times

A group of South County cities—Aliso Viejo, Dana Point, Irvine, Laguna Beach, Laguna Hills, Laguna Niguel, Laguna Woods, Lake Forest, Rancho Santa Margarita and Mission Viejo—argued strongly against the plans for a noisy airport near their cities.

After years of political battles, the South County cities stopped the plans for a big airport at the old El Toro Marine base.

Bill Campbell

*Supervisors Bill Campbell {center} and Tom Wilson*
*speak at an anti-El Toro Airport rally.*

Today, the City of Irvine is developing the old Marine base as a mix of houses, businesses, a college campus, and ambitious Great Park plans.

Miss Jones was describing the Great Park plans when Chris raised his hand.

"What about the spies and ninjas?" he asked.

Miss Jones patiently explained—once again—that there weren't any ninjas in Orange County. The spies were trained on Catalina Island, not at the El Toro Marine Corps Air Station.

However, she said, there were some secret spying activities in World War II–era Orange County.

One secret plan was to have helium-filled blimps patrol Orange County's starlit coastline after dark, silently searching for enemy submarines. The secret surveillance plan became a reality, but the blimps never found any enemy subs.

First American

*A huge World War II blimp hovers in the air with the gi-normous Tustin blimp hangar in the background.*

Miss Jones said the big spy blimps were housed in two huge all-wood hangars at the Santa Ana Lighter-than-Air Base in what is now the City of Tustin.

Six blimps could be stored in each huge blimp hangar. Each blimp was really big, she said, but the blimp hangars were even bigger. Much bigger.

When the blimp hangars were built in 1942, they were the largest clear span wooden buildings in the world.

Today, they still are still believed to be the largest wooden buildings on the planet.

Chris once saw the big blimp hangars through his car window when his family was driving along Jamboree Road in Tustin. He did not get out and look at them close up, but he could tell that the blimp hangars were really, really big.

Image via www.airfields-freeman.com

*A-4 Skycrafts fly in formation above the El Toro Marine Corps Air Station.*

They were gigantic, he thought.

Enormous.

Gigantic and enormous.

"GI-NORMOUS!" said Chris out loud, loud enough for everyone to hear him.

"Christopher, raise your hand if you have something to say," scolded Miss Jones.

Chris did not stop smiling. He was already day dreaming about the big blimps and the even bigger Tustin blimp hangars and what he had seen with his own eyes.

He knew what he thought.

Cool word, *gi-normous.*

*Santa Ana's Liberty Girl label was used before*
*World War I from 1910 to 1913.*

**Hector G. Godinez**
**(1923-1999)**

A national civil rights leader, Hector Godinez was the U.S. Postal Service's first Mexican-American district manager and a prominent Orange County elected official.

The Santa Ana High graduate was a decorated World War II hero, a tank commander who won a Bronze Star for combat bravery.

After the war, he worked 48 years for the post office, rising from a humble clerk's job to a top west coast leadership position.

He helped found the Santa Ana Chapter of the League of United Latin America Citizens (LULAC) in 1947 and by 1960 was the civil rights group's national president. He also was an elected trustee of the Rancho Santiago Community College District.

The Hector Godinez U.S. Postal Service Processing Center in Santa Ana and Hector Godinez Fundamental High School are named in his honor.

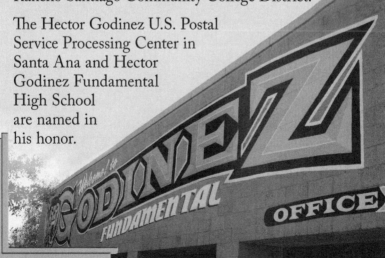

# 23 The MAGIC MOMENT

Orange County's magic moment came on July 17, 1955.

On that hot summer Sunday, Disneyland opened in the City of Anaheim, right next to the Santa Ana Freeway (I-5).

Millions of people from all over America watched on their black-and-white television screens—color television was not available in those days—and saw Walt Disney's Magic Kingdom. They were **enchanted**.

After seeing Disneyland on television, children everywhere dreamed of visiting the theme park called "The Happiest Place on Earth."

In that one magic moment in 1955, Orange County became a world-class tourist **destination**.

Everyone in the classroom was paying close attention as Miss Jones talked about the day Disneyland opened and today's Disneyland Resort.

She brought in some big photographs of Disneyland Park and California Adventure and Downtown Disney. Almost everyone knew something about Disneyland, but they did not know the Magic Kingdom was more than 50 years old.

"It is hard to believe now, but a lot of people thought Disneyland was a big gamble when it first opened in 1955," Miss Jones said. "There had never been anything quite like it, and no one knew if it would be popular or not."

Disneyland, of course, was an instant success. Miss Jones said more than one million guests drove out to Walt Disney's Magic Kingdom in the first few months it was open. Today, 10 to 12 million guests visit Disneyland every year.

Chris was annoyed as Miss Jones rattled off the numbers. He didn't know why she did it.

He decided to ask.

*Walt Disney inspects the 1954 construction of Sleeping Beauty's Castle.*

"Why all the numbers?" he asked, trying not to sound snotty. "Why not just talk about Disneyland?"

Miss Jones could tell by the somewhat pained tone of Chris's voice that he was serious. She knew this was not one of his far-out questions about ninjas or cows.

Chris really wanted to know why she always used numbers, dates and **statistics**.

"Christopher, numbers can help explain things to you or provide you with a better understanding of what I'm talking about," she said, looking right at him. "You know that if something is ten times bigger than something else, it is much, much bigger.

The biggest selling food at Disneyland is ice cream

"So if I say Disneyland had one million guests in 1955 and ten million today, you know that many, many more people are going to Disneyland today than used to go there."

Chris was listening. He understood what she was saying. But why did she always use so many numbers?

Miss Jones smiled. She asked Chris if he remembered talking about panning for gold at Knott's Berry Farm and when he brought in his little vial with gold in the bottom.

"I remember," Chris said.

Miss Jones asked, "Did you bring in your gold to share it with everyone and to provide some proof that your story was true?"

Chris said that was exactly what he did.

OC Indian Guides began in 1966 in Mission Viejo

"Your bottle was proof—or evidence—that your story was true," Miss Jones said. "You knew most people would believe your story, but more people believed you when you brought in some proof."

She looked away from Chris and spoke to the entire class.

"Numbers and statistics are a way to provide proof—or evidence—that something is true," she said. "I know you believe me, but I like to use numbers and facts to prove to you that I really know what I'm talking about."

Chris thought about what Miss Jones was saying. It made sense, but he always believed her anyway. She didn't have to prove anything to him.

Chris suddenly flashed on a new thought: Maybe he trusted Miss Jones because she was always providing little bits of proof or evidence. He had never noticed she was doing it.

He was thinking about proof and evidence and trusting Miss Jones when he realized the teacher was talking about Orange County being a world-class tourist destination.

"When tourists fly into John Wayne Airport or drive on our freeways, they visit Disneyland, Knott's Berry Farm, the Crystal Cathedral, the Mission San Juan Capistrano and the beautiful beaches along our 42 miles of coastline," Miss Jones said. "We have tourist attractions every where."

Laura Hoffman

*A bronze statue of movie star John Wayne towers over the John Wayne Airport terminal.*

Chris smiled.

Forty-two miles of coastline, he thought.

Miss Jones was providing just a little bit of evidence to prove that she knew what she was talking about.

The teacher could have just mentioned beautiful beaches, Chris thought. She did not have to say there were 42 miles of coastline, but she did.

No wonder he trusted her.

*This 1928 Western Lithograph features a genie and the magic of oranges.*

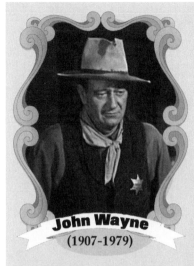

**John Wayne**
(1907-1979)

In 1979, the Orange County Board of Supervisors named the county's airport after Newport Beach–based movie star John Wayne.

Supervisors said they honored John Wayne because he symbolized America's patriotic values in both his films and his strong personal and political beliefs.

A broad-shouldered, 6-foot, 4-inch former USC football player, John Wayne played a movie hero in more than 150 films, many of them big box-office hits set in the Old West.

He won the Academy Award® as Best Actor for his 1969 portrayal of cranky one-eyed Marshal Rooster Cogburn.

A nine-foot tall bronze statue of John Wayne, dressed in a cowboy hat and boots, and wearing a six-shooter on his hip, stands today in John Wayne Airport's main terminal.

# 24 Mr. Million & MORE

Holding a paper with a lot of numbers on it, Miss Jones told the class that after World War II, Orange County changed forever.

She said numbers told the story: After the war, in 1950, there were 216,000 men, women and children living in Orange County.

By 1960, the county's population more than tripled, to over 703,000 people.

Derek Debano

Three years later, on September 30, 1963, Orange County's 1,000,000th resident arrived at Anaheim's Martin Luther Hospital.

Newspapers said newborn baby Derek Debano was *Mr. Million*—Orange County's one millionth resident. The lucky baby was

*Derek Debano—Mr. Million*

showered with presents, his parents were honored at a big **civic** luncheon and business and political leaders said that beautiful baby Derek was a **symbol** of all that was good about Orange County's **phenomenal** growth.

Derek was celebrated for a few days in the fall of 1963, but *Mr. Million* was quickly forgotten as Orange County's population continued to grow bigger every day.

In 1980, two million people were living in Orange County. Today, more than three million people live in the nation's sixth largest county.

Brea's Micah Cullings is Orange County's Mr. Three Million

Miss Jones said that all the new people squeezed orange groves and lima-bean fields out of Orange County. Farming gave way to new homes and new businesses.

Looking up from her paper, Miss Jones said the county's growth was mind-boggling.

Chris agreed. His mind was boggled, all right, but not in a good way.

He wasn't sure what Miss Jones was talking about.

She said the numbers told the story, but he didn't know what story she was telling.

While Chris was grumping, Miss Jones folded her page of numbers in half, and continued talking about what she called Orange County's go-go growth.

She said that soldiers and sailors and Marines from all over America had been introduced to Orange County's mild Mediterranean climate and cool ocean breezes when they were stationed here during the war.

"Many of the World War II **veterans** who were stationed here wanted to live here," Miss Jones said, "but, to live here, they needed to find a job."

The veterans wanted jobs in the booming electronics, **aerospace**, scientific instruments and defense industries. They found good-paying jobs—and found a way to get to work—when freeways came to Orange County.

The first Orange County freeway—Interstate 5, the Santa Ana Freeway—came into Orange County in the 1950's, about the time the county's population began its spectacular growth.

Over time, Interstate 5, sometimes called "the I-5," was built from the Los Angeles County line to the San Diego County line. In some places, the freeway followed the same path that trailblazers like Francisco de Ortega and Gaspar de Portolá first took in 1769.

"The county's phenomenal growth depended on the I-5," Miss Jones said. "It was the freeway that people took to work in the morning and then took back home every night."

She said the I-5 became Orange County's Main Street.

*Lines of traffic jam Interstate 5, Orange County's Main Street.*

Miss Jones unfolded her page of numbers, looked at it for a moment, and said that in the 1980s, 50 percent of all of the people who lived in Orange County and two-thirds of all of the county's jobs were within three miles of the Santa Ana Freeway.

"That's impressive," Miss Jones said.

That's just another bunch of numbers, Chris thought. He forgot the numbers as soon as he heard them, but one thing stuck: He remembered that the Santa Ana freeway—the I-5—was Orange County's Main Street, the road that went from one end of the county to the other.

Orange County's Main Street, Chris thought.

Pretty cool.

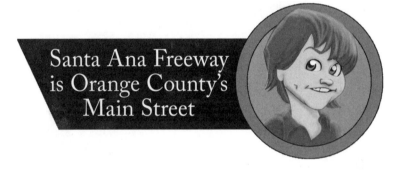

Santa Ana Freeway is Orange County's Main Street

When Chris refocused, Miss Jones was talking about other freeways and toll roads and how the OCTA's Measure M program rebuilt the county's freeways.

She paused, and then asked if anyone knew what grew next to freeways.

"Graffiti," Chris said, "and scraggly trees."

Miss Jones frowned and told Chris to raise his hand before he spoke.

The teacher said shopping malls grew next to freeways.

"Orange County did not have any big shopping malls before the freeways were built," she said. "After the freeways were built, shopping patterns changed and car-friendly shopping malls popped up next to the new freeways.

© 2011 South Coast Plaza. Used With Permission

*School children see South Coast Plaza being built in 1966.*

"It became easy for people to hop in their cars and drive to the new, freeway-friendly shopping malls," said Miss Jones. "Shopping at the malls in Orange County became a form of recreation as well as a shopping experience."

In 1966, cousins Harold and Henry Segerstrom, the grandsons of pioneer farmer Carl J. Segerstrom, built Orange County's most glamorous

*Harold Segerstrom*

shopping center—the glitzy South Coast Plaza—on the Segerstrom family dairy next to the brand new San Diego Freeway (Interstate 405).

South Coast Plaza is now one of the world's greatest luxury shopping centers.

Alana Cacciatori

*The painted horse from a carousel is the trademark of Costa Mesa's South Coast Plaza.*

The gi-normously successful, 280-store South Coast Plaza often is featured in television programs where everyone is rich and beautiful and wearing **elegant** clothes. It is part of Orange County's growing **sophistication**.

Chris was kind of getting what Miss Jones was talking about.

He learned that after World War II, new people and new houses and fancy new shopping centers replaced orange groves and lima-bean fields, just like family farms and big-time agriculture once replaced the county's Old West cattle ranches and vast sheep-grazing lands.

Chris got it. Over time, things change. Freeways and shopping centers and new jobs caused big changes, just like irrigation water and farming once caused big changes years before.

Things change.

Chris didn't know if he liked it, but he got it.

Author's Collection

*A butler brings a tray of oranges to a gentleman with refined tastes – an epicure.*

**Henry Segerstrom**
**(1923-present)**

Henry Segerstrom is a managing partner of C.J. Segerstrom & Sons, developer and operator of South Coast Plaza, one of the world's greatest shopping centers.

He also helped create the magnificent Segerstrom Center for the Arts, a 14-acre performing arts complex built on land donated by the Segerstrom family. In August 2000, he gave $50 million, the largest charitable cash gift in Orange County history, to the performing arts center.

The Segerstrom Center for the Arts today is larger than New York's famed Lincoln Center.

A decorated World War II Army Artillery Captain, Henry Segerstrom also served for 30 years as an elected director of the Orange County Water District.

Segerstrom High School and Segerstrom Avenue honor Henry Segerstrom and his distinguished family.

# 25 A NEW Rhyme

Miss Jones reached into her desk and pulled out a bright red ballcap with a big, red, embroidered letter *A* on it. There was a little white circle—a little halo—sewn around the top of the cap's big letter *A*.

Miss Jones put the cap on her head and then asked, "Who knows what this is?"

Hands shot up everywhere in the room.

Chris's hand went up immediately. He knew exactly what was on the teacher's head. He had a cap just like it at home. He wanted to shout out his answer.

Miss Jones called on Katie instead. Chris was disappointed, but Miss Know-It-All knew what was perched a little sideways on Miss Jones' head.

"It's an Angels baseball hat," Katie said. "It's the kind of hat baseball players wear."

The teacher said Katie was correct. Miss Jones added that the red ballcap—and the Angels baseball team— were important parts of Orange County's national image and also marked an important milestone in Orange County's local history.

Baseball was the national pastime, Miss Jones said, and when the Angels left Los Angeles for Anaheim, everyone believed Orange County was moving into the big leagues of business, **commerce** and national recognition.

Anaheim Public Library

*In 1965, the famous Big A symbolized Anaheim Stadium.*
*Today, the ballpark is called Angel Stadium.*

"Things were moving very, very fast in those days," Miss Jones said. "The Santa Ana Freeway and Disneyland arrived in 1955. Cal State Fullerton, Orange County's first big college, opened in 1959. *Mr. Million*—Orange County's 1,000,000th person—was born in 1963.

"And," Miss Jones said, "after discussing Orange County's fabulous future with Walt Disney, Gene Autry decided to move his big league baseball team here in 1965."

Like the Angels, big aerospace, aviation and **electronics** companies were moving to Orange County. Smaller suppliers and specialty companies followed the big businesses.

Business boomed in the 1960s and 1970s. Jobs were growing faster than the county's population. And the highest profile business to move from Los Angeles to Orange County was Gene Autry's California Angels baseball team.

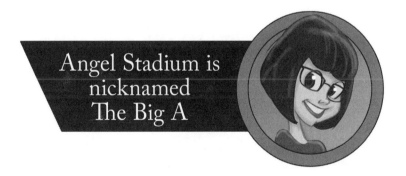

Angel Stadium is nicknamed The Big A

The Angels move generated tremendous publicity for Orange County. Sports pages throughout the nation began running the Anaheim **dateline** for Angel home games, reminding people across the nation about Orange County.

And, in those days, outspoken Orange County news makers were featured in national newspapers almost every day.

Miss Jones said Orange County community leaders, like berry farmer Walter Knott, scientist Arnold O. Beckman and movie star John Wayne, were well-known for their super-patriotic, conservative political views.

Conservative politicians also made their mark. In 1950, she said, a young Yorba Linda–born Republican attorney named Richard M. Nixon was elected as a U.S. Senator from California.

Two years later, he was elected Vice President of the United States.

OC Archives

*Walter Knott in front of his replica of Philadelphia's Independence Hall*

When Richard Nixon became vice president, California Governor Earl Warren chose another Orange County Republican, Thomas H. Kuchel, the grandson of Anaheim pioneer Conrad Kuchel, to serve in the U.S. Senate.

For eight years in the 1950s, the Vice President of the United States and the influential U.S. Senator from California were both from Orange County.

"Many people were surprised to learn that two of the best-known Republicans in America—Dick Nixon and Tom Kuchel—were from the same California county," Miss Jones said. "Both politicians were very well known nationally, but it was Mr. Nixon who went on to greater fame and higher office."

*Richard Nixon*

*Tom Kuchel*

Chris thought that neither politician was as famous as the red letter *A* embroidered on Miss Jones' ball cap.

The Angel ball cap did not fit the teacher very well, but Chris thought it was kind of cool that she was wearing it and it was awesome that she was talking about the Angels.

Still, Chris was trying to figure out why Miss Jones was talking about baseball teams moving to Orange County and about big-time politicians appearing in national newspapers all the time.

He guessed that she was saying that as Orange County grew, it became big-time, too.

Hey, Chris thought. That rhymed.

He tried it again.

> *As Orange County grew,*
> *It became big time, too.*

Chris liked it. It would be easy to remember.

And it rhymed a lot better than orange and door hinge.

*Los Angeles's Western Lithographers*
*created this label about 1946.*

**Gene Autry**
(1907-1998)

Gene Autry was known as "the Singing Cowboy" on the radio, in the movies and on television.

His hit songs include the holiday favorites *Rudolph the Red Nosed Reindeer* and *Frosty the Snowman*. His theme song was *Back in the Saddle Again*.

In 1941, he was so popular that a small Midwest town voted to rename itself Gene Autry, Oklahoma. He has five stars on the Hollywood Walk of Fame, more than any other celebrity.

In 1961, he bought a brand-new Major League baseball team, the Los Angeles Angels. Four years later, he renamed his team the California Angels, moved the team to Anaheim and put Orange County in the big leagues.

In Anaheim, he was honored when Gene Autry Way, a street leading into Angel Stadium, was named for him.

# 26 The 37TH President

Katie sat on the edge of the big outdoor fountain with water **cascading** behind her, waiting for the Richard Nixon Presidential Library and Museum to open.

She was bored.

Katie's mom was taking her and her little brother, Niko the Nikosaurus, to see the museum and to walk through the little wood house where a president of the United States was born.

Katie knew former President Nixon came from Yorba Linda. When he was president, he lived in a seaside mansion in San Clemente that he called *Casa Pacifica*, or the "House of Peace."

Katie's mom told her those things as they drove to the museum. Besides that, Katie didn't know anything about Richard Nixon.

Inside the museum, Katie learned that Richard Nixon was a respected world leader, the American president who eased world tensions by visiting China. He was the president who talked about "Peace with Honor" as a way to end the Vietnam War.

When the Saigon government collapsed and fell to Communist military forces at the end of the Vietnam War, millions of Vietnamese **refugees** streamed out of their native land.

Many of the Vietnamese refugees moved to Garden Grove, Stanton and Westminster.

Kirsten Mack

*Little Saigon has become one of Orange County's most vibrant business areas.*

Over time, the Orange County area known as Little Saigon developed shopping malls, fine restaurants and thriving businesses, many of them along Bolsa Avenue.

Little Saigon soon grew beyond Bolsa Avenue and became home to more Vietnamese people than any other place outside of Vietnam.

Katie liked that President Nixon wanted to help the Vietnamese people who were loyal to America during the Vietnam War. She liked that he visited China to promote world peace. She liked that he called his home the "House of Peace."

*Yorba Linda native Richard Nixon speaks to a hometown rally in 1952.*

When Katie walked though the little hand-built farm house where Richard Nixon was born, she felt a little proud that a Yorba Linda farm boy who lived in such a humble home could grow up to be President of the United States.

But there were other stories about Richard Nixon that disturbed her. She heard he was the only president in American history to resign. Some said he was a crook and a **scoundrel**.

The reasons Richard Nixon quit as President in 1974 sounded very, very bad. He was accused of approving dirty tricks, including burglary and hiding illegal listening devices called "bugs" to spy on his political enemies.

Prosecutors said the President ordered his assistants to lie, to hide the truth and to cover up crimes.

Many of the President's top aides went to jail during what was called the Watergate scandal, but Richard Nixon was never prosecuted. Instead, he resigned and was given a special **pardon** by Gerald Ford, the man who replaced him as president.

The first passenger on Disneyland's Monorail was Richard Nixon

The conflicting stories about Richard Nixon were confusing. Katie wasn't sure what to believe.

Katie felt she needed to know more about President Nixon before she decided what she thought about him. When she knew more, she would make up her own mind.

Until then, no one would bamboozle Katie. Not even Richard Nixon.

Katie was thinking about President Nixon when her mom went in to the museum's gift shop, trying to buy a book and trying to control Niko the Nikosaurus. While her mom tried to shop, Katie poked around a little.

Disney©

*The Nixon family on the first monorail ride with Walt Disney watching and television personality Art Linkletter peeking out of the top*

She looked at Richard Nixon's picture and autograph on golf balls, notepads, water bottles, pencils, pens, shot glasses, coffee cups, postcards, books, chapstick, mouse pads, key chain and decks of playing cards.

Katie saw a copy of the Declaration of Independence printed on a tan tee-shirt and a maroon tee-shirt with the letters WWND on one side and *What Would Nixon Do?* on the other side.

She also saw some nice-looking shirts for little kids, one with "Future First Lady" on the front and another with "Future President" on the front.

She looked at those shirts for a long time.

When Katie's mom was ready to leave, Katie had a question.

"Why," Katie asked, pointing at the shirts, "would you want to be a Future First Lady when you could be a Future President?"

Katie's mom did not answer, but she had a big smile on her face.

"We've got to go," she said.

*The Frances Citrus Association was named after James Irvine's wife, Frances Plum Irvine.*

**Richard M. Nixon**
**(1913–1994)**

In 1968, Orange County native Richard M. Nixon was elected as the 37th President of the United States.

Born in Yorba Linda, he attended local schools until 1928, when he transferred from Fullerton High School to Whittier High.

Before he was elected President, Richard Nixon served as a California congressman, a United States senator, and as Vice President of the United States under President Dwight D. Eisenhower.

While he was President, Richard Nixon worked at the White House in Washington, D.C. and also at his San Clemente home. Some called his Spanish-styled home in Orange County the *Western White House.*

**Bedeviled** by political scandals during his second term, Richard Nixon resigned as President in 1974.

The Richard Nixon Presidential Library, Museum, birthplace and gravesite in Yorba Linda are national monuments.

# 27 Olympic Goose Bumps

Chris wasn't very interested in politics or politicians, but he liked it when Miss Jones talked about sports.

Somehow, when she talked about Orange County's famous sports teams, it didn't seem like schoolwork. It didn't seem like work at all. It was actually kind of interesting.

Miss Jones said that big-time professional sports teams—like other big-time businesses—came to Orange County as the number of people in the county grew.

The Angels came first, playing their first games in Angel Stadium in 1966, a little after Orange County's population topped one million people.

In 1980, when there were just about two million people in Orange County, the Los Angeles Rams professional football team moved here.

In 1993, as the county's population topped two-and-a-half million and was building to today's three million people, the Mighty Ducks brought professional hockey to Anaheim.

As Miss Jones talked about sports teams, Chris was surprised to hear that the Walt Disney Company, the giant entertainment company that owns Disneyland, once owned the Angels and the Ducks, too.

The Walt Disney Company owned the Anaheim Angels in 2002, the year the team won the World Series and was the best baseball team on the planet.

*Anaheim celebrates as the Angels baseball team wins the 2002 World Series.*

The Mighty Ducks were named after a Disney movie about an underdog peewee hockey team. When Disney sold the hockey team to high-tech businessman Henry Samueli, he dropped the "Mighty" from the team name and called his team the Anaheim Ducks.

Miss Jones said the Angels and the Rams and the Ducks were Orange County's biggest pro sports teams, but none of those big-time professionals were involved in the county's biggest sports **spectacle** ever.

In 1984, Orange County was a part of the 23rd Summer Olympics, a worldwide sports competition that brought together 140 different nations.

*Supervisor Harriett Wieder carries the 1984 Olympic Torch.*

Peter Ueberroth, a Laguna Beach businessman, led the Olympics. He did such a good job that *Time* magazine named him the 1984 worldwide Man of the Year.

"Los Angeles was the official host of the '84 Olympics, but the Los Angeles Olympics committee used locations all over Southern California for the international games," said Miss Jones. "Athletes from all over the world came here to compete as friendly rivals.

"For one brief, shining moment," she said, "the Olympic ideals of peace, brotherhood and friendship through sport came together right here."

Miss Jones said she saw some Olympic events on television and she saw some of the events in person. She saw part of the international Olympic Torch Relay with her own eyes.

"To start the Olympic games, a torch was lit in Greece and carried by a relay of runners all the way to the Los Angeles Coliseum," she said. "Famous people and ordinary people took turns carrying the torch across America. People lined the streets to see the torch pass by.

"It was very exciting and very emotional," she said. "People were on the streets laughing, cheering and waving flags. For the first time in my life, I heard patriotic people on the street chanting 'U-S-A! U-S-A!' as the torch passed by."

Miss Jones paused and, with what looked like a sparkle in her eyes, smiled at the class.

Courtesy of the City of Mission Viejo, California Heritage Committee Collection
*Families wave American flags at the 1984 Olympic Cycling Road Race in Mission Viejo.*

"I still get goose bumps when I think about it," she said quietly.

The teacher added that a number of exciting Olympic events were held in Orange County. The Anaheim Convention Center hosted wrestling matches. More than 100 bicyclists from all over the world raced along a 120-mile road course on the streets of Mission Viejo. Coto de Caza hosted the modern **pentathlon**.

California State University, Fullerton (CSUF), was the **venue** for team handball, a European sport kind of like soccer, but where players throw a ball with their hands rather than kick a ball with their feet.

Miss Jones said Cal State Fullerton was an excellent Olympic venue.

She said Cal State Fullerton, built on land that was once some of Charles C. Chapman's old orange groves, has an outstanding athletic and academic **tradition**.

With more than 37,000 students, it is the largest public university in Orange County and has one of the largest student enrollments in the nation. In 2009, only five colleges in America awarded more college degrees to Hispanic students than Cal State Fullerton.

"It is a university that reaches out to everyone," Miss Jones said.

CSUF has nationally recognized programs in business, communications and theatre arts.

Laura Hoffman

In sports, Cal State Fullerton has won 12 national championships in seven different sports.

*Cal State Fullerton is Orange County's largest college.*

Cal State Fullerton is only one of Orange County's many fine universities, she said.

Alana Cacciatori

*A seated statue of Charles C. Chapman is at the main entrance of Chapman University.*

Chapman University, a private college named after Charles C. Chapman, the King of Valencia Oranges, can trace its rich heritage back to 1861.

In 1954, the Los Angeles-based college moved to the City of Orange. Over time, Chapman's George Argyros School of Business and Economics thrived, a law school opened and programs in film, religion and theatre arts won national recognition.

With about 6,000 students, Chapman University is Orange County's largest private college. In sports, Chapman has won six national championships and is the only Orange County college with an intercollegiate football team.

Chapman University is **affiliated** with the Disciples of Christ church, Miss Jones said. Orange County has other church-affiliated colleges, including Irvine's Concordia College, Costa Mesa's Vanguard University and Aliso Viejo's Soka University.

Miss Jones said that sports and higher education are key parts of Orange County life.

In 2010, Cal State Fullerton had 35,590 students

"The decisions by sports teams to play here and the success of our world-class universities in educating people here are symbols of Orange County's growth and maturity," she said. "They are indications of the county's steady progress."

Chris didn't know very much about growth or maturity or progress, but he remembered his own little verse:

*As Orange County grew,*
*It became big time, too*

Chris was thinking about his cool little rhyme when Miss Jones jolted him by saying "big time."

She was talking about a University called UCI and a billionaire named Donald Bren.

Miss Jones was saying they were big time.

Chris didn't know exactly what she meant.

He would have to wait to find out.

*Cute puppies were featured in this standard size 10" x 11" 1917 lithograph.*

**Arturo Moreno**
(1946-present)

Arizona billionaire Arturo "Arte" Moreno became major league baseball's first Hispanic club owner in 2003 when he bought the Anaheim Angels.

He disappointed many sports fans in 2005 by renaming his team the *Los Angeles Angels of Anaheim,* but he overcame the name-change controversy by fielding championship-caliber baseball teams.

Under his leadership, Angel home attendance has consistently topped 3 million fans a year.

Arte Moreno is a Vietnam-era Army veteran and was once the CEO of a major billboard company. He was a part owner of the Phoenix Suns professional basketball team and owns Los Angeles AM radio station KLAA 830.

In 2009, he bought a showplace home in Corona del Mar.

# 28 Defining BIG TIME

Katie was trying to find a big-time joke.

She wasn't doing very well.

She read her joke book. She listened to her friends. She asked her dad for help. Nothing she heard was very funny.

She kind of liked a joke she heard on an episode of *iCarly*.

On television, Carly's brother Spencer asked, "What's the difference between roast beef and pea soup?"

The answer: "Anyone can roast beef but no one can pee soup."

Katie thought it was funny, but she did not like telling pee jokes. It did not seem right.

She was not going to tell Spencer's joke, even if some kids like that pain-in-the-pants Chris would think it was funny. She was going to find something better.

Katie was still thinking about finding a big-time joke when Miss Jones began talking about Irvine.

The teacher said that today the Irvine Ranch was one of the largest master-planned communities in the world, a huge area that was designed to balance homes, schools, parks, high-tech businesses, apartments, green industries and great places to shop.

Plans for the huge ranch began to take shape in the 1960s with a unique centerpiece: a 1,000-acre University of California campus.

The Irvine Company, the owner of the Irvine Ranch, gave the state the land for the University of California campus as part of the company's long-range development plans.

The 1,000-acre gift of land was more than four times larger than the Cal State Fullerton campus.

Author's Collection

*At the 1964 UCI dedication: (left to right) UCI Chancellor Dan Aldrich, President Lyndon Johnson, University of California President Clark Kerr, Supervisor Cye Featherly and California Gov. Edmund G. (Pat) Brown*

On January 20, 1964, U.S. President Lyndon Johnson took a helicopter to a rolling hillside north of Newport Beach and formally dedicated the university called UCI.

Miss Jones said that having the president, a Democrat, fly into Orange County to dedicate UCI in the heart of a very Republican county was a very big deal.

University of California, Irvine

*UCI's Nobel Prize Laureates: Chemists F. Sherwood Rowland and Mario Molina (1995), Physicist Frederick Reines (1995) and Chemist Irwin Rose (2004)*

Almost immediately, UCI became a world class science school. Over time, UCI scientists won **prestigious** honors, including Nobel Prizes in chemistry and physics and big awards from the National Science Foundation.

While UCI was growing, the Irvine Ranch changed owners for the first time in 100 years.

After a long, ugly fight, the Irvine Company was purchased in 1977 by a team that included developer Alfred Taubman, automobile tycoon Henry Ford II, real estate developer Donald L. Bren and heiress Joan Irvine Smith, James H. Irvine's granddaughter.

Katie perked up. She had heard of Henry Ford. Her mom drove a Ford minivan. And she remembered Miss Jones talking about James Irvine.

But Miss Jones said it was developer Donald Bren, and not Henry Ford II or any of the others, who eventually took control of the vast Irvine Ranch.

Bill Campbell

*Donald Bren:*
*A developer with a vision*

Donald Bren had a vision for the great ranch. He wanted to improve on the old 1960s Irvine Ranch master plan by building a new type of Orange County community.

He balanced homes with **high-rises** and apartments, donated more than 50,000 acres of his land for public open space, focused on creating a world-class quality of life and supported education at every level.

He is generous with his money. No one has given more money to UCI than Donald Bren.

In 2006, the *Los Angeles Times* called him the most powerful man in Southern California. The federal government honored him for his **conservation** efforts. *BusinessWeek* magazine named him one of the nation's most generous philanthropists.

"Donald Bren fits the definition of big time," said Miss Jones. "Not everyone likes everything about him, but his vision has shaped Irvine, much of South County and parts of Newport Beach, Laguna Beach, Tustin, Orange and Anaheim Hills.

"His **imprint** has been placed firmly on the county for all time," she said. "His Orange County legacy is unmatched."

*UCI Entrance*

Chris listened carefully as Miss Jones talked. This Bren guy was big time, Chris thought. Really big time. Chris worried that he would have a hard time remembering enough about the guy if his name came up on a test.

Chris relaxed when Miss Jones added one last thing about the billionaire businessman.

"When we have a local history quiz later today, there will not be any questions about Donald Bren or UCI or any of the other things we talked about today," she said, "but we will cover many of the other things we've talked about."

Miss Jones smiled.

"Are you ready for the quiz?"

*These high-stepping white horses defined Hi-Class
in this 1929 Valencia orange label*

**Donald L. Bren**
(1932-present)

Real estate tycoon Donald Bren's vision of master-planned communities has shaped much of modern Orange County.

First as the developer of Mission Viejo and then as owner of the Irvine Ranch, Donald Bren has built communities that balance high-quality homes with excellent schools, public open space and world-class commercial centers.

In 2009, *The Times of London* named him one of the world's top eco-barons—one of the most environmentally sensitive billionaires on the planet.

A celebrated philanthropist, he gave UCI the Bren Events Center (and its famous anteater statue), Bren Hall and the Donald Bren School of Information and Computer Science. The Claire Trevor School of Arts at UCI is named for Donald Bren's Academy Award®–winning stepmother.

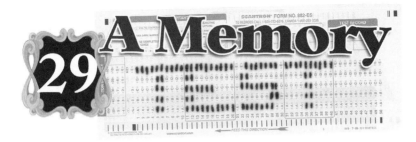

# A Memory

Here is the 10-question local history quiz, plus two extra credit questions, that Miss Jones gave to Chris, Katie and their class. Do you know the answers?

1.  Where do you live? (Write your answer on each line.)

    Country: _____

    State: _____

    County: _____

    Answers are discussed on pages 1, 2 and 3.

Circle the correct answer for each of the following questions.

2.  What was the name of the whale fossil found on a Laguna Niguel hillside?

    a.  Hippolyte

    b.  Joaquin

    c.  Junípero

    Answers are discussed on pages 9 and 10.

3. The fortune hunters who came to California during the Gold Rush were called:

   a. The Padres

   b. The 49ers

   c. The Angels

   The answer is discussed on page 48.

4. Who did not have an Orange County city named after him?

   a. Phillip A. Stanton

   b. Henry Huntington

   c. Andy Anaheim

   d. Richard Henry Dana, Jr.

   Answers are discussed on pages 43, 141 and 159.

5. The first woman to register to vote in Orange County was:

   a. Harriett M. Wieder

   b. Ellen F. Smith

   c. Jean O. Pasco

   The answer is discussed on page 123.

6. As Orange County grew, the county's Main Street became:

   a. Ortega Highway

   b. Interstate 5 (the Santa Ana Freeway)

   c. La Palma Avenue

   The answer is discussed on page 209.

7. To protect Orange County from floods, a big dam was built on the Santa Ana River in Riverside County. The name of the dam is:

   a. Prado Dam

   b. Don Pardo Dam

   c. Bicentennial Dam

   The answer is discussed on page 180.

8. The blimp hangars at the Santa Ana Lighter-Than-Air Base (now called the Tustin blimp hangars) are:

   a. The biggest glass buildings in the world

   b. The biggest wood buildings in the world

   c. The biggest Lego buildings in the world

   The answer is discussed on pages 192 and 193.

9. A magic moment in Orange County history was July 17, 1955, when what tourist landmark opened?

a. Knott's Berry Farm

b. Disneyland

c. Little Saigon

The answer is discussed on page 197.

10. Which President of the United States was born in Orange County?

a. Richard Nixon

b. Lyndon Johnson

c. Barack Obama

The answer is discussed on page 229.

Laura Hoffman

**Dr. Henry Samueli**
(1954-present)

A billionaire businessman, Newport Beach's Henry Samueli is a world leader in broadband communications technology. He is a named inventor on more than 50 patents.

An engineer and scientist, he is a co-founder of the Irvine-based Broadcom Corporation and, with his wife Susan, he owns the Anaheim Ducks Hockey team.

Henry and Susan Samueli also fund a charitable foundation that promotes science, technology, engineering and math in schools. UCLA's Henry Samueli School of Engineering and Applied Science, UCI's Henry Samueli School of Engineering and the Segerstrom Center for the Arts' Samueli Theater are named in his honor.

When the Anaheim Ducks won the Stanley Cup in 2007, Henry and Susan Samueli were enshrined on Anaheim's Walk of Stars.

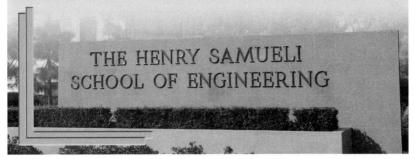

THE HENRY SAMUELI
SCHOOL OF ENGINEERING

Lee Berry was mad.

"The test wasn't fair," Lee said. "It was too hard. It covered too much. It wasn't fair."

Lee didn't usually complain, but he was whining now.

"Look at these questions," Lee said, holding the local history quiz. "You had to know the name of a dam in Riverside. You had to know the day Disneyland opened. No one knows that stuff. It's too hard."

Miss Know-It-All, who got every quiz question right, did not say anything. Katie just listened as Lee complained. After awhile, she started walking away.

Chris usually agreed with anyone who said any test was too hard, but Chris got every quiz question right, too. He didn't have anything to complain about.

Chris didn't want to argue or act like a Know-It-All, but he thought Lee was wrong.

"I didn't think the test was so hard," Chris finally said. "It seemed fair to me."

Lee did not react well. Soon Chris and Lee were talking loudly. It was not a friendly conversation.

Lee said Chris was a big-mouth who didn't know anything. He said Chris was even wrong when he said that nothing rhymes with orange.

Chris was wrong then and he was wrong now, Lee said.

At that moment, Katie decided to stick up for Chris.

"Chris was right when he said nothing rhymes with orange," Katie said.

Lee and Chris both looked at her.

This was unexpected.

"That's not right," sputtered Lee, looking at Katie. "It can't be right. You're the one who found the un-rhymable word. You did. You said door hinge rhymes with orange."

Katie looked at Lee like he was a gross little insect.

"Listen to yourself, Eel," Katie said with an annoyed edge to her voice. "Door hinge. Orange. They don't rhyme. They come close, but they don't rhyme any more than purple rhymes with burp hole."

Lee didn't know what to say. His eyes bulged a little and his mouth opened. You could see his tongue. Lee did not know what to say next.

Katie knew what to say.

"Awk-ward," she said in a funny voice.

While Lee was busy being confused, Chris realized that Katie saved him. She didn't have to, but she did. She did something really nice.

Chris wanted to thank her, but he was embarrassed to thank a Know-It-All, especially a Know-It-All girl.

As Lee walked away, Chris knew what he had to do. Chris looked down at his feet and said, "Thanks, Katie."

It was the right thing to say, the right thing to do. It was embarrassing, but he thanked her.

Katie smiled. She knew Chris wasn't always a pain-in-the pants. Sometimes he was lame or told dumb jokes, but she knew he was really nice. He was kind of smart, too.

After Katie stuck up for Chris, she did not feel like she needed to tell any dumb jokes to impress him or anyone else. She quit worrying about finding a really funny joke.

She decided to just be herself, even if some people thought she was a Know-It-All.

After all, she liked being a Know-It-All.

She was proud that she knew things no one else knew.

She smiled.

She also knew a lot of things everyone else should know.

They should know that nothing rhymes with orange.

# Orange County Timeline

**1769**  Gaspar de Portolá's expedition enters what is now Orange County.

**1776**  Mission San Juan Capistrano is dedicated by Father Junípero Serra.

**1835**  Author Richard Henry Dana, Jr. and the brig *Pilgrim* sail into what is now Dana Point Harbor.

**1850**  California becomes the 31st state in the Union.

**1857**  Anaheim, Orange County's oldest city, is founded.

**1870**  Westminster Colony founded by Presbyterian Pastor Lemuel Webber.

**1875**  The Southern Pacific Railroad reaches Anaheim. Two years later, the big locomotive steams in to Santa Ana.

**1876**  James Irvine becomes sole owner of the Irvine Ranch.

**1889**  Voters carve Orange County out of southeast Los Angeles County. Santa Ana becomes the county seat of government. About 13,500 people live in the new county.

**1893**  The Southern California Fruit Exchange, later known as Sunkist Growers, organizes in Fullerton.

**1901**  The Old County Courthouse, then Orange County's tallest building, opens in Santa Ana.

**1905**  Balboa Pavilion built in what is now Newport Beach.

**1905**  The *Santa Ana Register*, which later became the *Orange County Register*, begins publication.

**1913**  Future President Richard Nixon is born in Yorba Linda.

**1918**  Nelson Holderman of Tustin becomes a national hero when he is awarded the Congressional Medal of Honor for his combat bravery in World War I.

**1919**  Charles C. Chapman, the King of Valencia Oranges, strikes oil in Placentia.

**1931**  Oilman Edward L. Doheny donates more than 40 acres of beachfront land to the state, creating California's first state beach near Dana Point.

**1934**  Walter Knott begins selling his wife Cordelia's specially seasoned chicken dinners at Knott's Berry Place.

**1940**  The U.S. Census shows Orange County has 130,760 residents.

**1942**  World War II–era military bases at El Toro, Costa Mesa, Seal Beach, Santa Ana, Tustin and other Orange County locations support the U.S. war effort.

| 1952 | Los Alamitos race course opens. |
|------|--------------------------------|
| 1953 | National Boy Scout Jamboree is held on the Irvine Ranch. |
| 1954 | Santa Ana Freeway (I-5) opens through west Orange County, creating new jobs and bringing in new people. |
| 1954 | Chapman University (then Chapman College) moves to the City of Orange. |
| 1955 | Disneyland opens in Anaheim. |
| 1956 | The era of orange crate art ends when citrus ranchers begin using cardboard boxes. |
| 1959 | California State University, Fullerton (then called Orange County State College) admits its first students. |
| 1963 | Orange County population tops 1 million people. |
| 1964 | President Lyndon Johnson dedicates the University of California, Irvine (UCI). |
| 1966 | Los Angeles Angels of Anaheim (then called the California Angels and later called the Anaheim Angels) move to Anaheim Stadium (now called Angel Stadium). |
| 1966 | Orange County's first Indian Guides program starts up in Mission Viejo. |
| 1967 | South Coast Plaza, one of the biggest luxury shopping malls in the world, opens in Costa Mesa. |
| 1967 | California Governor Ronald Reagan dedicates the terminal at Orange County Airport. |
| 1968 | Orange County native Richard Nixon is elected President of the United States. |
| 1970 | On a countywide vote, an Orange County bus system is authorized. |
| 1971 | The National Municipal League selects Placentia as Orange County's first All-America City. |
| 1979 | Orange County Airport is renamed to honor Academy Award®-winning actor John Wayne. |
| 1980 | Rev. Robert Schuller's Crystal Cathedral, the largest religious structure in California, opens in Garden Grove. |
| 1981 | Orange County population tops 2 million. |
| 1983 | Donald Bren becomes sole owner of the Irvine Ranch. |
| 1984 | Olympic events are held throughout Orange County. |
| 1986 | Orange County Performing Arts Center opens. |
| 1993 | The Honda Center (then called the Arrowhead Pond), home of the Anaheim Ducks (then called the Mighty Ducks) professional hockey team, opens in Anaheim. |
| 1994 | Orange County government declares bankruptcy, the biggest government bankruptcy in United States history. |

1994 President Bill Clinton and former presidents Gerald Ford, Jimmy Carter, Ronald Reagan and George H.W. Bush attend Richard Nixon's Yorba Linda funeral service.

1996 The $7.4 billion Orange County Pool Settlement, one of the largest bankruptcy settlements ever, is approved. Orange County government quickly emerges from bankruptcy.

2001 Disney's California Adventure opens next to Disneyland.

2001 Aliso Viejo, Orange County's 34th and newest city, is founded.

2002 The Anaheim Angels win the World Series of professional baseball.

2003 Orange County's population reaches 3 million when Micah J. Cullings is born in Brea.

2004 Plans to develop Orange County's last great ranch, the historic Rancho Mission Viejo, are approved by the Orange County Board of Supervisors.

2006 New York architect Ken Smith starts designing the City of Irvine's planned Great Park as part of the re-development of the closed, 4,700-acre El Toro Marine Corps Air Base.

2007 The Anaheim Ducks win the Stanley Cup, the world championship of professional hockey.

2010 Builder Donald Bren gives 20,000 acres to the County of Orange, completing his 50,000-acre gift of permanent open space.

2010 SpongeBob SquarePants, the cartoon character created by Savanna High School graduate Steve Hillenburg, a former marine biologist at Dana Point's Ocean Institute, wins an Emmy for best animated television program.

# Glossary

**Adobe** – Bricks made with mud, clay and straw
**Adjusted** – Arranged to fit perfectly
**Aerospace** – Business designing and building rockets, missiles and spacecraft
**Affiliated** – Connected or related
**Annoyed** – Irritated or bothered
**Aqueducts** – Canals or concrete channels that move water a long distance
**Archaeologist** – People who study humans and animals that lived long ago
**Astonishing** – Amazing or surprising
**Astrolabe** – A sailor's ancient navigational device
**Aviators** – People who fly airplanes or aircraft
**Bamboozled** – Deceived by trickery
**Beatified** – Being honored as Blessed by the Roman Catholic Church
**Bedeviled** – Bothered or given big trouble
**Bicentennial** – A 200-year anniversary
**Boldface** – Thick, dark lettering usually used for emphasis
**Building codes** – Laws or rules for construction of houses or structures
**Cathedral** – A big, elaborate church
**Cascading** – Large amounts flowing down
**Citrus** – Oranges, lemons and grapefruits
**Civilize** – To tame wild, savage behavior
**Civic** – Involving citizens and the larger community
**Commerce** – Involving business or finance
**Commercial** – Involving business or finance
**Commotion** – A noisy disturbance
**Community** – A group sharing a cultural or historical background
**Concentrate** – To think about closely or focus attention
**Conquistadores** – Spanish word for conquerors or armed military men
**Conservation** – Preserving and protecting natural resources, including rivers and forests
**Constitution** – A government's basic laws and governing principles
**Convenient** – Easy to use and comfortable
**Cornucopia** – A mythical goat's horn with a never-ending supply of fruits, grains and vegetables; sometimes called the Horn of Plenty

**Dateline** – The place where a newspaper story happens

**Debris** – Something that's been broken up and thrown

**Deployed** – Putting military troops in the right place

**Desperados** – Spanish word for Old West bad men

**Destination** – Predetermined place a person wants to go

**Diplomats** – Men or women who represent their countries in important talks and meetings

**Disasters** – Tragic events, often involving loss of life or great damage

**Disciplined** – Focused and firmly under control

**Disincorporation** – To stop being a city, usually by a public vote

**Droughts** – Long periods of hot, dry, rainless weather

**Electronics** – Businesses making devices using electricity like televisions, computers or cameras

**Elegant** – Gracefully refined and dignified

**Enchanted** – Charmed or magical

**Espionage** – The act and art of spying

**Evidence** – Proof of facts or information

**Exhibit** – A display or place to show things

**Fictionalized** – An imagined version of events

**Flattery** – Excessive praise

**Flourished** – Thriving and growing successfully

**Fossils** – Traces of living things from the prehistoric past

**Friar** – A member of a religious order

**Fugitive** – A runaway, sometimes from law enforcement

**Gawked** – Stared in disbelief

**Gobbledygook** – Words that do not make sense; nonsense

**Griped** – Complained or whined

**Heritage** – Something passed on from the past to the present day

**High-rises** – Tall buildings with many floors

**Imprint** – A lasting mark

**Incorporated** – A way to organize a business or government with special legal protections

**Influential** – Exerting authority over another person or event

**Investors** – People who make money by putting money in a business

**Irrigation ditch** – A trench dug to supply dry land with water

**Irrigation water** – Water used for farming

**Journal** – A personal record or diary

**Jurisdiction** – Area of authority, usually legal authority

**Legacy** – Something of value given to future generations

**Magnificent** – Great or splendid

**Manufactured** – Made by machines or special hand tools

**Mediterranean climate** – Sunny, dry summers and rainy, but not snowy, winters

**Military** – Involving the armed forces, especially soldiers and armies
**Mischievous** – Causing trouble in a playful way
**Missions** – Places where Catholic priests taught religion and Spanish ways
**Misiónes** – Spanish for missions
**Mumbled** – Speaking in a low, unclear way
**Nautical** – Anything involving sailors, ships or the sea
**Organize** – Arrange in a neat, well-planned way
**Pardon** – Official forgiveness, usually by a government official
**Pentathlon** – Athletic contest with five events
**Petroleum** – A type of mineral-rich crude oil found in the ground
**Phantom** – A dream image or ghost-like creature
**Phenomenal** – Exceptionally amazing or astounding
**Philanthropist** – Someone who does good deeds, often involving gifts of money
**Presidios** – Forts where Mexican or Spanish soldiers lived
**Prestigious** – Very important and well respected
**Profits** – Money made from a business
**Prohibitionist** – Someone who wants to stop the sales of alcohol or liquor
**Prominent** – Outstanding; standing out from the rest
**Promoting** – Advancing or supporting an effort or program
**Prosecutes** – Takes legal action against a person accused of a crime
**Prospered** – Succeeded financially
**Protested** – Complained or demonstrated against a law or action
**Pueblos** – Spanish or Mexican cities or towns
**Rancheros** – Owners of Spanish or Mexican ranches or farms
**Ranchos** – Spanish or Mexican ranches
**Ransacked** – Plundered, pillaged or looted by thieves
**Rebels** – People who resist unfair authority or go against normal rules
**Refugees** – People escaping bad conditions, usually for their own safety
**Replica** – An exact copy
**Ruffians** – Tough, lawless bullies
**Saloons** – Businesses or taverns that sell liquor, usually by the glass or mug
**Scoundrel** – A dishonorable villain
**Segregating** – Separating, often by race or ethnic origin
**Sewage** – Waste matter that passes through sewers
**Sophistication** – Cultivated, worldly good taste and manners
**Spanglish** – Spanish spoken with some American-English words or phrases
**Spectacle** – A dazzling display or exhibition
**Squirmed** – Twisted or wriggled uncomfortably
**Statistics** – Numerical facts or information

**Stone Age** – A prehistoric time of stone tools and primitive living

**Strategy** – A group of plans used to achieve a goal

**Strict** – Stern and precise enforcement rules and regulations

**Survival** – Something that continues or endures, usually under difficult circumstances

**Swashbuckling** – Acting as a dashing show-off

**Symbol** – Something used to represent or illustrate something else

**Taxes** – Money charged by the government to pay for government services

**Tradition** – A long-established custom

**Tragedy** – A great loss or disaster

**Transactions** – Business dealings between two or more people, usually involving buying and selling

**Trolley** – A streetcar or cable car running on a railroad track, usually in a city

**Twilight** – The time just before dark, the end of daytime

**Tycoon** – A businessman with a lot of money and influence

**Unusual** – Different or out of the ordinary

**Uprising** – A violent disturbance

**Utopian** – Idealistic but impractical goal

**Valid** – Legally binding and true

**Veterans** – People with experience, usually military experience

**Venue** – The place where an action or event happens

**Vineyard** – A place where wine-making grapes are grown

**Windjammers** – Sailing ships powered by the wind

**Zoning** – Government rules on how land or property may be used

# Index

271

# ACKNOWLEDGEMENTS

Some parts of a collaborative effort like *Nothing Rhymes with Orange* come from unanticipated sources, but the heart of this project comes from a very predictable place.

Generations of local historians, including Jim Sleeper, Spencer Olin, Don Meadows, Pamela Hallan-Gibson, Leo J. Friis and Phil Brigandi have done valuable research on Orange County's colorful past. This volume builds on their work. The bibliography is a very short summary of useful Orange County books written by able local historians.

The look of this book comes from Dan Almanzar's delightful illustrations. One of this project's great pleasures was conspiring with Dan as he brought the text to life. His work shines on every page.

Throughout this project's development, Tesoro Publishing's Chris Lowe and author Gail Eastman were quick to share their ideas and experiences. Chris's decision to use original photographs by XinaCat's Laura Hoffman and Bellissima Photography's Alana Cacciatori was a key to showing how local history really is alive all around us. Having German pancakes with Chris, Gail and Dan at the Original Pancake House in Yorba Linda also is a part of this project I genuinely will miss.

Many historic photos used here were tracked down by Jane Newell of the Anaheim Public Library, Don Tryon and Gwen Vermeulen of the O'Neill Museum and Bob Blankman, steward of First American's fine photo collection. Jim Hastings at The Enlarger in Santa Ana always provided a helping hand.

Special thanks go to Orange County Clerk-Recorder Tom Daly for keeping the history-rich County Archives open during tough financial times. And thanks to Archives Director Jean Pasco and her capable team of Susan Berumen and Chris Jepson, aided and abetted by the keen eyes of local historian Phil Brigandi and bon vivant Irwin Schatzman, for reviewing the manuscript and offering constructive clarifications and corrections.

275

Thanks to Orange County Superintendent of Schools Bill Habermehl, one of Orange County's finest public officials, for his upbeat introduction. Bill's deep personal commitment to our kids' education is evident in everything he does. His Department of Education Staff, including Judy Allison, Betsy Arnow, Rachel Dome, Rocio Vitko, Joan Perez and Debbie Granger, offered help and valuable insight.

Early drafts of this project also were reviewed by Anaheim school teachers Jenny Hitchcock, Socorro Ament, Cecilia Roman, and Kathy Manulkin, a retired principal at El Modena's *La Purisima Catholic School*. They validated the project concept and offered practical suggestions on how to make *Nothing Rhymes with Orange* a better teaching tool. Lynette M. Smith of AllMyBest.net edited the text and corrected many technical mistakes. Tesoro's Vicki Green and Helen Butler of Helen Butler Graphics helped shape the final version of this project.

The best advice on the actions and attitudes of third graders, however, came from my wife Dee, our four sons, Dan, Steve, Andy and Joe, and their wives, Alex, Niki, Amber and Lindsey. They coached me on the way parents think and the way kids behave today. They also contributed generously to my vast collection of lame jokes and weak wisecracks. Joe (and my niece Kirsten Mack) also helped with photographs and The Stever, a part-time member of the Archives Crew, also made shrewd suggestions on story structure and provided uncommon insight into the language of children.

On a very personal note, my participation in this project was made possible by Dr. David Imagawa and his talented team at UCI, as well as Dr. Jason Zell, Editha Gutierrez, Young Lee, Linda Armendariz, Karen Moll and so many others. Thanks to all of you for what you have done for me.

In the first sentence of these Acknowledgements, I used the phrase *the heart of this project*. Yes, the heart of this project is my wife Dee, the smartest person I know, the center of our family and my trusted collaborator. She is the true heart of every project we get involved in.

Stan Oftelie
Anaheim, CA

**iii,** William Habermehl, OC Department of Education; **4,** Miss Jones holding photo, First American; **7,** Walt Disney, Library of Congress; Disney Way, Laura Hoffman; **10,** Wooly Mammoths, Alana Cacciatori; **11,** Joaquin drawing, Alana Cacciatori; **13,** Interpretive Center, Alana Cacciatori; **15,** Ralph Clark, Author's Collection; Clark Park entry, Alana Cacciatori; **25,** Gaspar Portolá relief, San Juan Capistrano Historical Society; Portolá Parkway Signage, Laura Hoffman; **33,** Junipero Serra, San Juan Capistrano Historical Society; Junipero Serra Road, Laura Hoffman; **43,** Richard Henry Dana, First American; Dana Point Harbor, Laura Hoffman; **51,** Walter Knott, OC Archives; Knott's Berry Farm Old Time Adventures, OC Archives; **59,** Madame Modjeska, First American; Modjeska statue, Anaheim Public Library; **67,** Don Juan Forster, San Juan Capistrano Historical Society; Forster Mansion, Joe Oftelie; **75,** James Irvine, First American; Irvine High Vaqueros, Joe Oftelie; **87,** Richard O'Neill, San Juan Capistrano Historical Society; O'Neill Park, Laura Hoffman; **95,** Arnold Beckman, Anaheim Public Library; Beckman High, Laura Hoffman; **105,** James McFadden, First American; McFadden street sign, Alana Cacciatori; **113,** William H. Spurgeon, OC Archives; Spurgeon Avenue, Joe Oftelie; **123,** Ellen F. Smith, Author's Collection; Vote Here sign, Almanzar Industries; **131,** Nelson Holderman, Author's Collection; Holderman Park, Laura Hoffman; **141,** Philip A. Stanton, First American; Stanton street, Alana Cacciatori; **149,** James H. Irvine, First American; Irvine Regional Park, Alana Cacciatori; **157,** Colonel S. H. Finley, Author's Collection; Finley Avenue, Alana Cacciatori; **165,** Gonzalo Mendez, Santa Ana Public Library; Rendition of Mendez vs. Westminster stamp, Almanzar Industries; **173,** Gaddi Vasquez, OC Archives; Peace Corps logo, Peace Corps; **181,** Prado Dam, Laura Hoffman; **183,** Charles C. Chapman, Fullerton Public Library; Chapman University, Alana Cacciatori; **195,** Hector Godinez, OC Archives; Godinez High, Joe Oftelie; **203,** John Wayne, Wikipedia; John Wayne Airport signage, Laura Hoffman; **213,** Henry Segerstrom, C. J. Segerstrom & Sons; Segerstrom High, Alana Cacciatori; **221,** Gene Autry, Anaheim Public Library; Gene Autry Way, Alana Cacciatori; **229,** Richard Nixon, Public Domain; Nixon library/ birthplace sign, Laura Hoffman; **239,** Arte Moreno, Los Angeles

Angels of Anaheim; Angel Stadium, Anaheim Public Library; **247,** Donald Bren, The Irvine Company; Bren Events Center, Laura Hoffman; **253,** Henry Samueli, Anaheim Ducks; UCI Henry Samueli School of Engineering, Laura Hoffman; **281,** Stan Oftelie, Chuck E. Cheese photo booth; **282,** Dan Almanzar, Chuck E. Cheese photo booth

All orange crate labels from A Slice in Time can be found at www.asliceintime.com.

# BIBLIOGRAPHY

Baumgartner, Jerome W. *Rancho Santa Margarita Remembered*. Santa Barbara, CA: Fithian Press, 1989.

Brigandi, Phil. *Orange County Place Names A to Z*. San Diego, CA: Sunbelt Publications, 2006.

Carpenter, Virginia. *The Ranchos of Don Pacifico Ontiveros*. Santa Ana, CA: Friis-Pioneer Press, 1982.

Cleland, Robert Glass. *The Irvine Ranch (3rd Ed.)*. San Marino, CA: Huntington Library Publications, 1962.

Cramer, Esther R., et al. (Eds.). *A Hundred Years of Yesterdays: A Centennial History of the People of Orange County and their Communities*. Santa Ana, CA: The Orange County Centennial, Inc., 1988.

Eastman, Gail. *Anna's Home by the River: A Children's History of Anaheim (2nd Ed.)*. Fullerton, CA: Tesoro Publishing, 2006.

Friis, Leo J. *Orange County Through Four Centuries*. Santa Ana, CA: Pioneer Press, 1965.

Hallan-Gibson, Pamela. *Dos Cientos Años en San Juan Capistrano*. Irvine, CA: Lehmann Publishing, 1975.

Lowe, Chris, and Roberts, Emily. *Elephant Rides for Free: A Children's History of Placentia (2nd Ed.)*. Fullerton, CA: Tesoro Publishing, 2004.

Meadows, Don. *Historic Place Names in Orange County*. Balboa Island, CA: Paisano Press, 1966.

Moon, Tom. *This Grim and Savage Game: OSS and the Beginning of U.S. Covert Operations in World War II*. Cambridge, MA: Da Capo Press, 2000.

Sleeper, Jim. *Turn the Rascals Out! The Life and Times of Orange County's Fighting Editor Dan M. Baker.* Trabuco Canyon, CA: California Classics, 1973.

Stephenson, Terry E. *Shadows of Old Saddleback.* Santa Ana, CA: Fine Arts Press, 1931.

Talbert, Thomas (Honorary Editor-in-Chief). *Historical Volume and Reference Works Including Biographical Sketches of Leading Citizens, Three Volumes.* Whittier, CA: Historical Publishers, 1963.

Walker, Doris. *Dana Point Harbor/Capistrano Bay: Home Port for Romance (4th Ed.).* Dana Point, CA: To-the-Point Press, 1995.

# PROFILES

# Stan Oftelie

Stan Oftelie is an Orange County original.

He was the first Chief Executive Officer of the Orange County Transportation Authority, served as the Orange County Business Council's CEO, and once led the Orange County Transportation Commission.

In the early 1970s, he was an award-winning reporter for the *Orange County Register* and the *Los Angeles Times*. He also served as Ralph B. Clark's Executive Assistant.

Stan earned two Master's degrees from the University of Southern California, one in journalism and one in public administration. He received undergraduate degrees from Arizona State University and Cypress College.

He was named Cypress College's Americana Man of the Year in 2000 and was chosen as the college's 1996 Alumni of the Year. In 2006, the Center for Regional Leadership honored him as one California's leading Civic Entrepreneurs.

Stan and his wife Dee, an Anaheim attorney, have been married more than 40 years. They have four married sons, all born in Orange County, and five grandchildren, all born in Orange County.

During the 1956-57 school year, Stan was a third grader at Buena Terra Elementary School in Buena Park. He was a good reader, but received bad marks in handwriting.

You can e-mail him at **Stan@oftelie.com**.

# Dan Almanzar

Illustrator Dan Almanzar has been drawing all his life.

He worked for the Walt Disney Company for 19 years and now is doing freelance work for Nickelodeon, Skechers' comic books, and others needing a skilled and inventive artist.

In 1990, Dan earned a Bachelor of Fine Arts degree from California State University, Fullerton with an emphasis on illustration. He currently lives in Yorba Linda with his wife Erica and their children Alana and Jacob.

In the 1980–81 school year, Dan was a third grader at Linda Vista Elementary School in Yorba Linda. He enjoyed drawing and cartooning, but did not do very well with his math facts.

You can e-mail him and look at other samples of his artwork at **www.danalmanzar.com**.

Animal _____

Book _____

Best friend _____

Color _____

Food_____

Place to visit _____

Song_____

Teacher _____

Thing to do _____

TV Show _____

When I grow up, I want to be_____

_____

If I were mayor for a day, I would_____

_____

# Ordering Books

Order Online
at
www.NothingRhymesWithOrangeBook.com

Tesoro Publishing
P.O. Box 528, Fullerton, CA 92836-0528
www.tesoropublishing.com